THE COLOR OF CITIES
AN INTERNATIONAL PERSPECTIVE

In praise of cities;
and for my progeny in the new century.

Library of Congress Cataloging-in-Publication Data

Swirnoff, Lois.
 The color of cities : an international perspective / Lois Swirnoff.
  p.   cm.
 Includes index.
 ISBN 0-07-063348-7
 1. Color in architecture. 2. Cities and towns. I. Title.
 NA2795.S93   2000
 711'.4—dc21   99-59189
                                                CIP

McGraw-Hill

*A Division of The **McGraw·Hill** Companies*

1 2 3 4 5 6 7 8 9 0   DOC/DOC   0 6 5 4 3 2 1 0

ISBN 0-07-063348-7

The sponsoring editor for this book was Wendy Lochner, the editing supervisor
was Stephen M. Smith, and the production supervisor was Sherri Souffrance.

Printed and bound by R. R. Donnelley & Sons Company.

McGraw-Hill books are available at special quantity discounts to use as
premiums and sales promotions, or for use in corporate training programs.
For more information, please write to the Director of Special Sales, Professional
Publishing, McGraw-Hill, Two Penn Plaza, New York, NY 10121-2298.
Or contact your local bookstore.

THE COLOR OF CITIES
AN INTERNATIONAL PERSPECTIVE

LOIS
SWIRNOFF

McGraw-Hill
New York San Francisco Washington, D.C. Auckland Bogotá
Caracas Lisbon London Madrid Mexico City Milan
Montreal New Delhi San Juan Singapore
Sydney Tokyo Toronto

CONTENTS

ILLUSTRATIONS

Photography by Lois Swirnoff

Also shown in "Colors Grouped by City." See page 224.

PREFACE

The dimensions of color are many. For the painter color is the primary sensory marker—direct, immediately expressive—and resonant with meaning. It shapes urban environments as well—a discovery made the first time I departed my native New York and experienced the visual impact of color in cities in Italy and Mexico.

Wherever color maps surfaces the effects are not superficial. Color affects environments, forming and transforming them. In towns and cities it confers magic to everyday life and experience. The quest to find and record city color began with travel, and in time, as I applied my painter's eye to the camera, the role of color in urban dimensions crystalized.

Local expression is vividly coded in the color of cities. Patterns of usage emerge, showing a universal syntax within the diversity of local vernaculars. Over time and distance, variations in urban color appear to be influenced by their geographic locations. Clearly, the quality and intensity of environmental light depends upon the angle of the Sun. But more fundamentally, perhaps, environmental light may prove to be a formative condition, to which the human visual sense itself adapts, or is shaped. Color sensitivity varies among cultures. City color in diverse parts of the world shows a distinct relationship between locale and palette, a variance in spectrum shaped by light.

A vital urban environment is one in which the visual elements—light, color, and architectonic form—signify and express civic functions. Although the virtual world of cyberspace offers us a powerful tool of communication, it cannot replace the influence of physical places. Cities are the matrix of civilizations. Formed over time, they embody and sustain human endeavor and cultural values; they shape us. Absent coherent, stimulating, and meaningful environments we risk becoming impoverished, alienated—and deprived.

Contact with a culture may entail the reading of its urban codes. To remind readers of the significance of cities, as exemplars of cultures and as rich and complex places, I suggest that they begin their adventure with direct sensory experience. I have found that color is universal expression, woven into the pattern of the urban fabric by people themselves.

The Graham Foundation in Chicago generously provided grants to support travel to Japan, enabling the inclusion of a significant Asian culture in this global study. In addition, the Foundation gave me the opportunity to return to Italy, where I was able to revisit Tuscany, Umbria, and Bologna to augment my visual memory with fresh documentation. For its significant contributions to this project, I am very grateful to the Graham Foundation.

Wendy Lochner, Senior Editor of Architecture and Design at McGraw-Hill, initiated the project, encouraging me to organize visual and written material for publication. I am indebted to her for her interest and support, and for providing the opportunity to present as much of the abundant visual evidence as possible in this volume.

I wish to thank friends and associates for their contributions: Phoebe Hoss gave helpful suggestions after reading a draft of the manuscript. Kathy O'Keefe made available to me the resources of the Lindgren Library at M.I.T. to check geophysical facts. The invaluable advice of graphic designers Paula Scher and Seymour Chwast helped me to shape the appearance and presentation of this book. And my collaborator in its design, Sarah Heckles, brought it to realization.

Lois Swirnoff
Boston, Massachusetts
January 2000

INTRODUCTION

Cities and towns are distinctive and unique. An urban explorer reads character in architectural style or urban form more frequently than by color, but these are perceptual patterns that stimulate the eye and enliven the human spirit. In their absence, the lack of aesthetic dimensions produces the monotonous achromatic environments familiar to many modern city dwellers.

Many cities in history, however, were designed with a sense of the significance of order and clarity, and sensitivity to perceptual patterning, in which color played a part. Italian cities, those of Venice, Rome, Firenze, Bologna, and the hill towns of Tuscany and Umbria are uniquely formed and distinctively colored. In Mexico and the Caribbean, color plays a role in shaping the urban environment, while vividly expressing the character and culture of its people.

As city form represents conceptual order, the plan of building volumes and spaces, city color shapes perceptual *experience*. A sense of color, in fact, may be a culture's least recognized, but most direct, visual signature.

Preferences are evident in the vernacular. People select colors in their surroundings, exhibiting a taste for certain combinations and avoiding others. A collective "eye" seems to guide these choices, rather than individual inclination. They are distinctive and self-contained, as much a part of human coding in cities as their signs and symbols.

Color is a direct expression and represents a visual response. Local and specific to place, it seems to arise within a particular environment, as languages do. A sensory parameter, the color sense is connected to other cognitive attributes; it can express meaning by association. Shaped by light, it may represent a response in people to the characteristics of the natural environment, to its harshness or abundance, desolation or luxuriance, relative presence or absence of sunlight. Color experience and color sense appear to be collective, vernacular expressions.

Light and color are fundamental characteristics. Light visually defines form, and color is physical. Over the Earth sunlight varies in its duration and intensity, a function of its angle of incidence. Thus, Stockholm's ambiance is pervasively subdued, even shadowy, compared with Jerusalem's.

The colors of cities are shaped by these elemental factors. The taste for highly saturated hues in Mexico may be expressed by the juxtaposition of lime green with magenta on adjacent facades, a combination that would wither the eye of an Englishman. Rather than ascribe these differences in culture to taste, "about which we do not dispute," I have found the issue a fascinating challenge, more likely determined by global location. Instead of considering its role as embellishment, additive or extrinsic to urban patterns, color may be regarded as a special attribute of form itself, a shaping or *trans*forming component.

Considering the limits of the range of sensations perceived as color by the human eye, the variety of their combination is astonishing. A limited group or range of colors can elicit immediate response in the human psyche, while representing the life and character of a people. Just as, by analogy, the traditional Japanese garden, given its small scale and limitation of careful placement, can concretely represent the universe.

Over a period of time I have photographed city color in countries located in different parts of the globe. The human impulse to embellish and enliven the surroundings appears to be universal. An expression arising from the place itself, color is applied to houses, to the facades of streets, on shops, in marketplaces and squares—wherever people dwell, carry out their transactions, interact with one another. The syntax of usage, interestingly, is similar from place to place, but color gestalt differs remarkably. Just as grammatic structures are embedded in languages, vernacular color usage is rule based, but its expression may be as diverse in the world as

are its spoken languages.

The language of color is based upon human perceptions of the visible spectrum. Red, orange, yellow, green, blue, indigo, and violet are denoted almost universally. Where a genetic mutation in vision causes achromatopsia, or total hue blindness, among the Pingelaps on an atoll in Micronesia, words for brightness and darkness denote where, on the continuum of light sensations, the hues, reflected from the environment but not seen, are classified. Inuits perceive and name, on the other hand, many more distinctions between whites than can any other culture.

Groups differ in their denomination of spectral hues as basic. Some designate red, yellow, and blue, others include black and white as primaries. One culture defines eleven, rather than the Newtonian seven, as basic colors, including brown and purple in the group. Cultures may differ in defining the primacy of sensations, but they recognize and consistently name similar hues in their color experience.

When cultural groups use color, therefore, it is the amount, quality, and chromatic intensity in colors that differ. French blue does not appear in Italian hill towns, and Italian ochers do not occur in Paris. Furthermore, colors appear different in different places, and generally do not travel well. Although brilliant dissonances in color juxtapositions appear vivid and stimulating in Mexico, under Manhattan's filtered light the same combinations may read as depressing. In an urban setting the color gestalt is a result of the quality of atmospheric light, and frequency and recurrence of groups of colors, quantitatively expressed.

The use of color for adornment in clothing, or ornamentation of the body, can be understood as self-enhancement and display.

Color usage in the habitat and immediate surroundings extends the sense of the individual's intimacy with the environment. The use of color in the city or place, however, is a collective expression. Extended to the urban field it no longer reflects personal or subjective choices; as it confers special identity to place it is a cultural marker. Over time, with repeated usage, certain color groups recur, becoming traditional preferences in human populations. By observing the differences among cultures in their color expressions, one can attribute them to the response of the "vernacular eye."

But what influences these particular choices in the first place? Is there a single prevailing factor—location on the Earth's surface? Is it a direct response to light, to the prevalence or absence of sunlight's intensity? Or can the coloration of the natural environment itself influence a mimetic response in the eye/brain? Does proximity to the sky in high plateau country, or to the ocean along coastal plains, significantly shape the light sense?

In this study, all of these factors seem to play a role. But as the Earth provides locales with tremendous variety and diversity of geographic and physical features, some of these factors predominate over others. Altitude predominates in the Alps, and latitude is more significant at the Equator. It does seem to be the case, however, that the environment—offering distinctive natural conditions—does shape human visual

I-2 Bay of Naples, winter

responses, certainly psychologically, and perhaps physiologically as well.

I have observed the role of color in the built environment to be a basic way to confer special identity to place. More than any other formal attribute, color represents a direct response to the particularity of the natural context, a human dialogue with the environment—a humane recording or responsive signature of its influence. This response, whether physiologic or psychological, can be complex. The flavor of places, like the flavor of wines or cheese, tends to be local.

Human sensitivity to light originates as a sensory response to the environment. Visual and tactile in essence, it may be related to other sensory factors such as taste and smell. For example, the grapes that produce great wines are dependent primarily upon geographic location; the chemical components of the soil, the range of temperatures, the intensity and duration of sunlight, the amount of precipitation—all are factors that influence the quality of the grape, and ultimately the taste of wine. True also of coffee, tea, and cheeses, the cultivation and development of unique ranges of tastes for the pleasure of the human palette is one of the hallmarks of civilization. Vini*culture* and agri*culture* are among the oldest forms of human activity, and a precious heritage. It makes us what we are.

A palette of colors, similarly, seems to be cultivated in places where human populations have been stable or continuous for long periods of time. The collective reaction to the environment appears to develop as an expression, after prolonged exposure of the eye and brain to the conditions of the environment, rather than representing self-conscious design or choice. The pervasive quality of light, whether intense or subdued, the complexity of hues in the volumetric color of bodies of water, and the chemical components of soils induce colors, and the clarity or translucency of atmospheres stimulate the visual system in complex and contradictory ways. Over time, I speculate, what people see in their surroundings they use. Percept becomes concept. The vernacular color sense arises as a collective human response to the environment.

Rather than being prescriptive, however, the responses represented by local color are varied, like vernacular dialects spoken in the world. For example, near the Equator, where the Sun's angle of incidence to Earth's surface is 90°, reflectivity of light is at its maximum. The reaction of the eye's retina to this intense stimulation is rapid, and the tolerance of individuals to unfamiliar levels of luminosity may be limited. Sunglasses or hats with visors are recommended to travelers. Natives adapt.

In Central Asia in the nineteenth century the migratory tribes of Khanates carried or wore the artifacts of their civilization. Portable yurts, or tentlike structures, were their habitats, an ingenious indigenous form of housing adapted to desert life. Under the stark conditions of desert light this group adopted the process of Ikat dyeing of fabric, an invention of the Central Asian cities of Samarkand and Bukhara. These were fashioned into garments of brilliantly colored reds, yellows, and deep indigos, in bold and striking patterns. A tradition that arose in the arid neutrality of harsh desert light, this human response—a restoration of bright color—may represent a need in

this circumstance as biological as that of thirst for water. The human retina can react to the stimulus of brilliant light by blanching out the receptor cells that respond to the rich saturation of hues. Bright or deeply saturated hues used in the environment restore balance to the visual system, as they offer the antidote or complement to the bleak monotony of the surroundings. The use of saturated color in habitat and garments may also represent the recall of seasonal phenomena—brilliantly colored desert blossoms—offering less transitory relief than flowers to the neutrality of desert expanses.

As a geographic marker, the color of cities reveals the global range and diversity of vernacular expression. This study is international, but its global scope is limited to those places that I have experienced in travel, namely, cities in the northeastern United States, Southwest, and West Coast; Mexico; the Caribbean; Italy; France; England; Scandinavia; the Alps; the Middle East; and Japan—a significant sample of the Earth's surface. Direct experience of these environments has been essential, where, literally, the atmosphere drawn by eye and breath and the light imbuing the places are felt, influence how they are seen.

The camera may extend the eye, and the photograph can correct the impression of memory by its graphic evidence. Some visual experiences elude the capacity of mechanical reproduction and the limitation of film emulsions. The photograph can be a record or visual imprint, enabling the recall of experience, a means of comparison for observation or study. To the artist photography is a medium used to create imagery. It was with hopeful expectation that all of these aspects would be addressed when I photographed these city images. In all cases the film was limited to Kodak Ectachrome or Kodachrome.

To make credible comparisons in this study, I framed diverse places with my lens to record the emerging patterns or attributes that recurred. These were:

1. **The Environment:** Features of the urban setting, the landscape, or bodies of water; natural characteristics of colors in place

2. **Light and Shadow:** The quality of light in places which shape the environment

3. **Spaces:** The configuration of the city—the presence or absence of open spaces; the proximity of buildings to one another; light and color in the piazza, arcade, or passageway

4. **Streets:** As spatial continua, the relationship of buildings to one another in their juxtaposition as colored facades

5. **Edges:** Essential boundaries between building and sky, or streets and water; distinctive urban features or silhouettes, such as the skyline of Manhattan or the canals of Venice

6. **Facades:** The color of individual buildings, domestic, commercial, or industrial (Graphic Facade: The colors of storefronts and their function as signage)

7. **Apertures:** Doors, windows, archways, marked characteristically by color

8. **Markets:** Local forms and color

9. **Materials:** Natural color sources—stones, marbles, adobe, brick, and pigments from soil sources

10. **Details:** Specific to place

Consequently, these attributes of form, compared in the cities discussed, are presented by category throughout the following chapters.

Light is the primary factor shaping perception of a place—a function of the angle of incidence of the Sun. Latitude or position of a city on the Earth's surface determines quantity of light. Iceland, for example, receives significantly less sunlight than Italy. Quality is similarly affected. The acute angle of incidence the more northern the latitude, elicits light's long wavelengths—the reddish ambers observed at sunset. Altitude influences the clarity and intensity of atmosphere and light. Meteorologic and climatic conditions, and complex geophysical events that influence the Earth and the eye in the appearance of color will be observed, if not explained, in the chapters that follow.

Of the cities studied here, those in Mexico combine highest altitude with latitude in proximity to the Equator, two factors possibly interacting to create the intensity of its environmental light. Notably, I have observed the use of fully saturated color to be greater in Mexican cities than in any other countries studied here.

Explanation of the complex geophysical factors conditioning these experiences are well beyond the purview of this study, but may suggest further rigorous scientific analysis.

To make general distinctions I have separated cities into three broad areas: cities or regions of light, median cities, and cities or countries in shadow. Defined by observation, these categories distinguish between places that, on average, represent environments in which ambient light is visually experienced as pervasively high, middle, or low on a relative scale of brightness.

Human color responses to the light of an environment are complex and unpredictable. In the sample of the globe represented by the cities studied, one can roughly see a spectrum, corresponding to their geographic locations.

THE CONTEXT: PHYSICAL PLACES

1

PERCEPTION OF CITIES

To its inhabitants the modern city is a mere backdrop, a neutral stage set to the theater of daily activities. Primarily utilitarian, city form, its streets, urban pathways, and transit systems exist to be used—the more efficiently, the better. In his/her haste to arrive at an appointment in time, to descend into the subway or catch a bus, the citizen is often oblivious to the surroundings. Observed casually, in passing, a store window or sign may emerge from the neutral blur; color may signal the eye as a detail at a bus stop, a useful spot of brightness, or arrest the attention in an advertisement, an inadvertent interruption. Occasionally perhaps, the sculptured detail on a lintel, the hasty view of a cornice overhead, or the flash of a well-mannered brass or copper plate on upper Fifth Avenue draws an aesthetic response from a Manhattanite's eye. The inattentive pedestrian may conflate all streets in great twentieth-century cities to a neutral anonymity, unaware of their distinctiveness. Manhattan's neighborhoods, despite commercial overdevelopment, are still visible, clearly distinguished by urban features, such as the scale and height of buildings in the East and West Villages, SoHo, NoHo, Museum Row on upper Fifth Avenue, and many small cross streets, where nineteenth-century scale and texture have not yet been obliterated from the urban fabric.

A city is best experienced on foot; the rhythm of human pace accompanies its perception by eye. A total sensorium, the city is experienced, not only kinetically and visually, but also by sound, smell, and, virtually, by taste. The acrid smell of tar attacks the back of the tongue, while the aroma of garlic may arouse the appetite. Too many stimuli, chaotically presented—too many screeching brakes, whining sirens, blaring boom boxes; too much disorder, squalor, stench; too much disregard for patterns in motion; invasion of personal space; uncivil behavior—alienate us. Turned off, we focus inward, preoccupied. The city becomes wallpaper, scarcely scanned by the eye, except to avoid obstacles or traffic in the path, and the essential link between human observers and their environment is severed.

How often is its famous skyline actually observed by the native New Yorker? Best seen while leaving the city, due north on Amtrak's rail, or from the window of a car from New Jersey, the remarkable profile is crowded, more a forest of buildings than the grand panorama it was in the 1940s and 1950s. Where is the sense that this great metropolis is situated on an island, in proximity to water on all sides, that it can be transversed readily east/west on foot? Even on the north/south axis, the major art museums along the Fifth and Madison Avenue corridors can be visited, if only briefly, on a day's walk. Some New Yorkers are rediscovering the sense of autonomy that accompanies walking to a destination, but the perception of most is that a ten-block walk will subtract too much time from the day. Perhaps because the urban pattern of Manhattan is so densely compacted, an individual's sense of scale becomes limited. In fact, the geography of this island is relatively small; the vertical scale of its built environment accounts for the sense of great size and lost time; waiting for elevators should be added to that of buses or trains to the crowded schedules of its inhabitants. Manhattan's urban rhythm is one of haste, then wait—but unlike a Gershwin tune— *un*syncopated.

This kinesthetic spatial sense becomes internalized. My perceptions of cities have been based upon the modality of the pedestrian. At that rate of speed facades are noticed, doorways and windows reveal their distinctiveness, the skyline emerges at intersections. More frequently than one thinks, the great pathways of the avenues can be observed, for example, from the less densely populated East Village uptown as one-point perspectives. Asphalt surfaces

gleaming in bright sun, at near distance, lead to buildings further along, framing an urban corridor vertically, to infinity. Near sunset, Nature reveals itself in the deepening blue sky framed by the zigzag of buildings, if one looks west toward the Hudson for a moment. The natural beauty of this arch-metropolis overcomes human chaos, and a connection with place is re-formed in that instant.

Los Angeles, at the continent's western edge, more a region than a city, is extended on all sides by the sense of an unlimited horizon. The county's edge is a coastline 80 miles long, from Huntington Beach north to Point Hueneme, of the expansive Pacific Ocean. Compact Manhattan is bounded by water, the Hudson River to the west and the East River are conjoined in the harbor, and open beyond to the Atlantic. The entire island is only 13½ miles long and 2½ miles wide. The feasibility of walking in New York is supported by its size and the regular grid of its street patterns, which conceptually organizes the space of Manhattan and makes it one of the most coherent places in the world to navigate. Los Angeles cannot be explored on foot. Kinesthetic experience of the city depends upon wheels and engine, and the linear configuration of hundreds of miles of freeway. Once internalized, the vastness of the sense of space tends to send Los Angelinos to their cars even in their local neighborhoods; here, after all, were born the drive-in bank and church.

The return to New York, my native city, after 14 years in Los Angeles caused a radical revision in my kinesthetic sense, and my consequent perception of Manhattan. Where, at one time, it seemed to be the greatest city in the world—it remains the most cosmopolitan—it now appears to be relatively moderate in size and high in density. This also makes it efficient. The proximity of services to the place of work, the mix of commercial and cultural enterprises—restaurants, museums, and concert halls adjacent to business districts—are urban patterns that evolve in old cities and cannot be easily matched by design. Perhaps the periodic rediscovery of New York as the world's capital is due to its spatial density.

The role of color in the urban scheme is linked to spatial/temporal perception. The modality of motion influences visual awareness of the city. The pedestrian's moving eye scans and selects, pauses in the continuum of a street to notice a feature, a storefront or graphic facade, a particular doorway. The scan, a fluctuating rhythm of figure and background, changes from day to day. Visual stimuli in the city are so rich they provide continuous variety and surprise—actively engaging the eye and brain. The stimulus of color occurs in the orchestration of connected facades on a street. A linear grouping, or cluster of colors, such as the purple-browns of Manhattan's nineteenth-century town houses, lends coherence to a brownstone neighborhood. Recurrence of these colors on adjacent streets confers identity to a district. A shift in intensity or hue draws attention to a single facade, isolating it as an individual building. Doorways and windows provide breaks in the uniform rhythm of facades, and are denoted as special by their color or detailing. These experiences of color usage are replicated elsewhere; they constitute a syntax for the color of old cities.

By contrast, the extended new city, taken in continuous motion by car, is more a *temporal*/spatial experience; the moving eye functions as running film in a camera. From the elevation of a freeway, districts are panoramas. Connected to their natural contexts, such as the Hollywood Hills, neighborhoods may be configured by mountains and canyons into discrete groupings of houses. In such domestic places individuality of styles prevail, and the vernacular eye may express its affinity with nature by imitating the coloration of vegetation, or of the semiarid environment itself. Hypothetically, from a freeway, clusters of colors, as pivotal markers, could arrest the attention of the moving eye and contribute to the isolation or articulation of groups of buildings in a district, if deliberately designed or organized. In a rapidly moving car, the scan of an immediate environment becomes a blur. Color foci, limited by near distance to landmarks or large building masses, would localize districts and lend coherence to them in the monotony of the extended urban field. The dynamics of order in new cities in the future may be shaped by the recognition that color, in groups of hues as patterns or clusters or recurring in depth/space, can confer a means of organization of the urban field in time as well as space.

THE SITING OF CITIES

Natural forces or features once provided the rationale for the establishment of cities. In ancient times some natural sites were considered sacred; a particular setting was chosen for its metaphoric and physical characteristics. By 2000 B.C., Vincent Scully asserts, the siting of Cretan palaces made deliberate use of landscape features, namely an enclosed valley in which the palace is set, a mound or conical hill on the north/south axis with the structure,

1-1 Temple, Segesta

and at a distance a double-peaked or cleft mountain. These forms, both natural and built, were fundamental to the creation and practice of ritual in Minoan civilization.

Earth/sky complementarity informed the siting of classical Greek temples. The Parthenon faces east, toward the rising Sun, perpendicularly on the morning of Apollo's feast day. Temples to Aphrodite were sited high, on the rise of a hill or atop a mound, in relation to the sea. At Segesta, the temple to Demeter is described by Scully as the nipple on the breast of the ancient mound. To the west the ground drops precipitously into a gulf, separating the temple site and a mountain. Thus the Minoan scheme of the mound, or conical hill, with the earth/cleft and double-peaked mountain, was carried into classical Greek

architecture as a profound and abiding human metaphor.

The architectural remains of aboriginal culture in the American Southwest are integrated also with their natural surroundings. The sacred city of Puye on the Santa Clara Reservation in New Mexico is located on a mesa, commanding the great horizontal sweep of landscape. One's eye level, meeting the peaks of distant mountain ranges, holds the boundary of the horizon. The individual is connected to the grandeur of the place, physically rooted, but soaring by eye scan; and there abides at this site an almost palpable sense of spiritual presence.

At Mesa Verde the Anasazi built their dwellings and ritual spaces into the conformation of rock and hill, a spectacularly sited city,

totally integrated into its surroundings. In Mesoamerica, at Teotihuacán, in Mexico, the pyramids were engineered with enormous precision on this ancient mesa to relate to the Sun.

The siting of cities on mesas in the ancient world had another function as well. Inaccessible mountain tables provided a natural defense; the city of Masada was a refuge for ancient Israelites from their Roman invaders. Cave dwellings in the cliffs and canyons of the Southwest inhabited by the Anasazi, or ancient ones, were concealed from the casual intruder, and some are found with great difficulty by archaeologists today.

When commerce replaced religion or ritual as cities' raison d'etre, they were sited at locations whose physical features were favor-able to shipping and docking. The city of Venice at its peak was the most cosmopolitan for its time and was a global center of commerce. Trade routes to and from Constantinople, India, Egypt, and Spain brought the islands of Venice not only great wealth, but also, via its lagoons, the materials with which its elegant palazzi were constructed: white marble from Istria, porphyry—even obelisks from Egypt— to adorn its piazzette.

In the seventeenth century on the American continent, Boston, before the extensive land-filling of the Back Bay, was an assemblage of islands. Its harbor provided the fledgling colony with an optimal natural setting for commerce with the mother country, Great Britain. It took 100 years before New York

1-3 Taos pueblo

1-4 Lower Broadway, Manhattan

Harbor developed to supersede Boston as an international city of trade. The natural features of Manhattan and Brooklyn, once separate cities, in their access to the Atlantic Ocean, provided steamships of greater size a better port. In consequence, New York replaced Boston as a great mercantile center.

If the function of the city in modern times has become increasingly utilitarian in the narrowest economic sense, rather than as an agora, sacred place, or human community, the existence of neighborhoods in great cities demonstrates that these deeper human requirements

persist and prevail. There is a link between the sensory aspects of environments and their habitability. Human beings congregate in cities to interact with one another in a great variety of ways; in schools, places of worship, libraries, museums, concert halls, and restaurants, as well as to govern, shop, and transact business. Aesthetics play a greater role in the urban fabric than is currently acknowledged. The sense of beauty is universal. For ancient civilizations ceremony, ritual, and polis were integrated tangibly into daily life in city form, expressed in architecture, art, music, and dance through the spatial, visual, auditory,

1-5 Parliament, London

landscape, proximity to bodies of water, and latitude and altitude form the context or visual environment. Natural settings, in turn, are part of a city's image and influence its appearance. Imagine Venice without its lagoons, Jerusalem without the hills of Moab, or San Francisco without its bay.

The perception of places, however, is more fundamentally influenced by the physical factor of light. The interplay of light and shadow, the primary tool of the painter for rendering volumes on the flat picture plane, is the basis for the perception of form, the environmental field itself. To the eye, the perceptual patterns wrought by sunlight define the volumes and spaces constituting the landscape, city, and figures in relation to the background, themselves the very stuff of vision.

The surfaces of buildings are articulated by light and shadow, and material details are exposed by the angle of incidence of sunlight to the surface of the Earth. Everywhere this angle differs; it changes seasonally and by diurnal rhythm. It articulates the soft, squat, mud forms of the pueblos of the Southwest, just as it carves the cast iron rhythms of columns in New York's SoHo. The filtered light of England produces a more evenly diffuse ambience. The perpendicular style of London's Parliament buildings delineate by their stone tracery, drawing the eye vertically by lineaments of contrasting material to express monumentality. Venetian urban spaces are medieval, confined, narrow; the dramatic contrast between labyrinthian passageways and open piazzette are orchestrated by shadows, and the brightness of the Sun imbuing the city is reflected in its canals and in the lagoons of the Adriatic.

and kinesthetic senses. Vernacular color may represent the simplest, most basic response of the human spirit to the absence of these real presences in the city and may symbolize an attempt at their restoration.

LIGHT, SURFACE, AND THE ENVIRONMENT

Conceptually good city form is defined by a distinctive plan, orderly patterns, articulate boundaries. Cities are shaped by their geographic features, the topography of the

1-6 Colonnade, Segesta in light

Color is shaped by light. Low levels of ambient light, as in London, are scattered and diffused by pervasive fog, a function of latitude and meteorology. The development of architectural linear style may be related to the filtered flatness of the light, when a relative absence of articulation in natural sun and shadow calls for greater definition in structure. The eye may also respond to the quality of the Sun's condition in its influence on color.

The bright green of England's grass, the con-

sequence of abundant moisture and dedicated gardening, is also a matter of visual adaption. Under low levels of luminosity the human visual system, the eye and brain, registers hues of middle wavelength such as greens, and short wavelengths such as blues and violets, as bright. Understated hues characterize London's and Cambridge's buildings. Deeply saturated, rather than bright colors, prevail as vernacular preferences; here they suffice to stimulate the eye.

Light, furthermore, is the physical source of color. Against the neutrality of the tufa columns on the remains of the temple at Segesta, in Sicily, warm daylight is reflected as yellow-amber-hued on one side of the cylinder, with cool blue-violet shown on its shadowed surface. As a general rule, shadows contain hues complementary to those of the light source. In the absence of coloration in the environment, light physically elicits color. In neutral natural environments, such as deserts or semiarid landscapes, the acute angle of sunlight at sunset, favoring long reddish wavelengths, imbues the visual field with unexpected splendor—heat for the eye as the atmosphere cools. In winter landscapes, white snow, brilliantly lit at noon by yellowish-white sunlight, contains vivid blue-violet shadows, where its surfaces are dimpled by footprints. In the most stark environments natural light presents color by polarization.

Light shapes the field in another sense in the subtropics. Here, where the Earth/Sun axis is more consistently near perpendicular, reflectivity approaches its maximum, and plant life thrives. Tropical plants, gorgeously variegated in their coloration grow to great size in the rain forests of Mexico. Flocks of parrots fly, as raucous in their plumed finery as they are in

1-7 Colonnade, Segesta in shadow

harsh desert light, but we are not blinded in the desert, or if so, only temporarily. Perhaps the light sense, the human eye and brain, evolved as the highly flexible and accommodating system that it is in response to the contradictory demands of the environment.

To observe a distant landscape, for example, is to notice that the contrast effect between objects' boundaries diminishes with increasing distance from the eye. At the same time, the entire visual field progressively increases in its luminosity to equal the intensity of the sky. To distinguish with clarity objects decreasingly visible under increasingly intense light means that the eye and brain have to reconcile the great discrepancies between these opposing tendencies. At the same time, under these conditions the appearance of colors remains relatively stable—astonishingly so. A red roof in a distant Meditteranean landscape remains red on a bright day, not pink, as the mitigating intensity of light might allow the eye to factor.

Tabletop scale models studied in my book *Dimensional Color* showed that light and shadow on simple volumes are proportioned by the visual system, rather than measurable by the reflectivity of their surfaces. I have come to think that the geometries of brightness in the environment are processed as ratios by the visual system to maintain relative consistency in appearance of volumes under differing conditions of light. This hypothesis may begin to explain the puzzling issue of color constancy, that is, the tendency of hues to retain their appearance under varied conditions of luminosity.

voice, and appear almost imprinted as flat shapes by their brilliant coloration against the sky. No wonder, then, that a taste for highly saturated color develops in the human population. Architecture in Mexican cities provides quintessential examples of vernacular color, as vivid, sensuous, and fully expressed reflections of the natural environment.

The question of the light sense itself arises as a fascinating paradox of adaption. The human eye and brain respond to a great variety of natural visual conditions. As the inhabitants of northern cities, we may be discomforted by

The environmental light of a place is conditioned by the angle of incidence of the

Sun. On a given day, a location plotted by the grid of longitude and latitude reflects its angle of incidence. Over the course of a year, this angle changes with the seasons. In the northeastern United States, for example, in Boston, the Sun appears low on the horizon in winter and higher in summer. On average, though, Boston receives less light than Barbados does, where, nearer to the Earth's Equator, the angle of incidence increases. At the Equator the Sun's angle is perpendicular to the Earth, and the reflectivity of its light is at maximum. These differences are primary influences on Nature's colors.

Oceans differ in appearance. The ranges of hues and their intensities are affected by the atmosphere, which is physically related as a system; by weather, season, time of day, and the rhythms of their motions. Highly complex, the Atlantic's range of steel-blues, cobalts, indigos, and grays, can be compared with the Southern Californian Pacific, with its chromatic ranges of ultramarine blue, blue-greens, deep greens, violets, and ochers. Both great oceans turn ocher or amber when the acute angle of the Sun rakes their surfaces. At the island of Barbados, the Caribbean Sea fluctuates in its coloration from minute to minute. Unstable, because light's reflectivity is unstable at this latitude, the color of the sea scintillates as it transforms itself, phenomena that transcend the film emulsion's capacity to render. The water is a variegated field, changing from depth to surface with hundreds of aquas, light cerulean blues, chrome greens, violets, and whites visible to the eye in rapid succession. The skies here are also richly hued in butter to lemon yellow, mauve to violet; the clouds are rose-pink to deep purple-violet as the Sun descends.

In the atmosphere, when light scatters, particles reflect the dominant wavelengths back to the eye. The sky is blue when these are at a shorter physical range. Landscape, the colors of soil, and vegetation reflect chemical and pigment to the eye. At great distances these combine and stimulate the retina. America's "purple mountains' majesty" denotes the scattered short wavelengths, violet-blues, that mix with and veil the reddish earth color of the hills. But in the Judean desert in Israel the atmospheric effects of light and desert produce a pink glow—the additive mix of yellow-amber sand and violet light yield a roseate hue, at once crystal clear and mysterious.

Altitude affects the lucidity of light and color. In the Alps the atmosphere is so clear that the eye will distinguish crisp boundaries between mountain mass and sky at great distances. In the desert, at sea level, atmospheric aridity, combined with intense reflectivity of light, can cause similar effects. Try hiking in the desert to reach a nearby mountain, only to find it seeming to retreat as the miles pass. Perceptual clues of the sharp edge to distance are seriously underestimated.

Mexico City, at an altitude of 7546 feet, has an atmosphere thinner than that of Vera Cruz at sea level. At one time the color of its sky was a deep cobalt blue, deeper, more saturated than any other in my experience, and darker than the surfaces of the city's facades. The dramatic juxtaposition of bright color and dark sky remains a vivid memory only. Today the gigantic city of Mexico has become so polluted that the sky is rarely visible as blue, but seen rather in the sickly hues of smog, a terrible testimony to Nature's vulnerability to human interference.

1-9 Atlantic Ocean, Martha's Vineyard

1-8 Cape Cod, winter

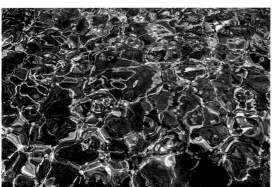

1-10 Red Sea, Israel

1-11 Dead Sea, Israel

1-12 Jericho, Israel

1-13 French Alps

2-1 Venice, view

URBAN SPACES:
CITIES OF LIGHT

The physical characteristics of cities—the site or setting, natural features of the environment that provide color and material, the quality of light—are basic, vital conditions of visual form. Variety in the configuration of city plans, open and closed spaces, lend distinctiveness to a conceptual pattern. The edge, skyline, shoreline, and foothill, as articulate boundaries, provide a sense of enclosure to a city's field. In rows of connected facades, color has a role to play as a variant among uni-*forms*. On facades or within districts, sculpted details provide embellishment, scale, or narrative imagery. These general urban features occur in Venice, archexample of the integration of form and color.

VENICE, ITALY

The city constructed on a hundred islets in the Adriatic Sea, mainly on wooden pilasters, is literally suspended between the ocean and atmosphere. The floating vision of a phantasmogorical city is the image created from the distant approach by sea, where the configura-

2-2 Domes of San Marco, Venice

tion of palazzi, campaniles, domes, and open piazze form a horizontal continuous band, separating sky and water. Richness and complexity of effect increase with proximity, as dazzling light is displaced by the material color of the surfaces of buildings and their patterns become more distinctive. Venice is urban throughout—all is built form; within the city only the presence of water and sky are natural. It is the richest, most complex human artifact extant; in its totality a colossal work of art.

Seen from the Campanile in the Piazza di San Marco, the streets below form the pattern of a dense labyrinth, intersected by ribbons of canals. Roofs made of red Meditterranean tiles lend consistency of coloration to the Byzantine complexity of building masses. In close proximity to the Campanile, the Byzantine domes of San Marco, one large and four smaller hemispheres forming the Greek cross, bring the complex, crowded urban rhythm to a pause. The Cathedral forms a visual pivot from above, and its open piazza, called "the world's largest outdoor living room," anchors the space. On foot, the Piazza di San Marco can be approached from all directions; the narrow passageways of surrounding streets empty out to its largesse. Viewed from up high, the piazza is a trapezoid; at ground level it appears to be a rectangle; the forced perspective of a

2-3 Piazza San Marco

colonnade enhances the illusion of distance from the cathedral's facade. At all times, in any weather, three orchestras perform simultaneously in the cafés lining its perimeter. As in other Italian cities, this great monument is functional, built for the use of people, not the archives of history.

Smaller piazzette are distributed throughout the city. The nearest is perpendicular to San Marco's and aligned with the Ducal Palace. Framed by two sculptured columns, it provides a gateway to the open sea, or, from the approach to the city, a ceremonial aperture. Colored tiles line the pavement, and those of the Ducal Palace, of alternating pink

2-4 Ducal Palace

2-5 View of Venice from the Campanile

2-6 Canaletto's view of the Grand Canal

2-8 Rialto Bridge

2-7 Central Market, Venice

jasper and malachite, and gold leaf remain that once adorned these surfaces; now, larger areas of painted facades predominate. In democratic manner, the heights of palaces are similar, and their apertures are framed by the signature style of the Venetian Gothic, but their faces shift from green-ocher to pink to mars yellow—colors of oxides; color, not form, creates the distinctions between them.

The piazza, a feature of Italian cities in general, are ubiquitous in Venice. Occurring throughout, these are small and variously shaped, providing marketplaces and public forums, none as grand as that of San Marco's. The Central Market is approached through an arch, and is covered with a wooden corbeled Renaissance roof, as elegant architecturally as are the domestic buildings.

Bridges shape the city image; the Rialto, most notably, is recognized as a Venetian icon. Small iron bridges cross canals, connecting streets throughout their meandering flow patterns. Walking through these spaces is an experience so richly varied that one's own rhythms are guided and choreographed, slowed to the pace of eye scan when the facades and details reveal their surprises—the pace of Ruskin, who described virtually every stone, and its colors. As with other great works of art, the visual experience of Venice is fully revealed only after patient observation.

and white patterns confer the roseate glow that greets a debarking visitor.

The urban pattern, a dense labyrinthian meander, pervades the island; the ubiquitous canals weave throughout the city, shaping its image and delineating its neighborhoods. The human habitat is discovered on foot; distinctive districts, built throughout its long history, remain. Along the Grand Canal the Canaletto view, downstream to Santa Maria della Salute, exists intact, appearing as it did in the eighteenth century. Here the great and wealthy elite constructed their palazzi. Traces only of the marbles, alabaster, porphory,

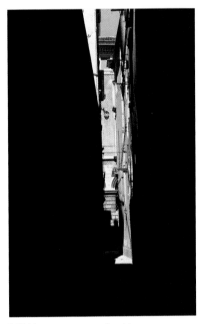

2-9 Venetian street

2-10 Venetian street near San Marco

2-11 Canal

City structures—some streets so narrow that they force pedestrian passage in single file—create shadows in the brilliant ambience of light and color. Buildings, settling on their rotting pilasters, are reinforced by and connected with arches. These add an urban rhythm unique to Venice. Arcaded passageways occur frequently, leading from street to street to the open space of a piazzetta. Like great frames, these archways articulate areas that, like pictures, become fixed in visual memory. They function also to provide shade and shelter from rain.

Colors, painted and layered over time imbue these places with warmth. The shadows cast are eloquent and shapely projections, mixing "illusory" with "real" forms. Although it is dense, the urban texture does not appear crowded. Narrow streets and passageways open into piazze. There is continuous byplay between light and shadow, and color—green ochers, clays, buffs, bisters, rose ochers, Lombard reds, soft blacks, near whites,

ranges of umbers, and siennas in hundreds of varieties. And throughout is woven the color of the canals, an organic green one can smell, unique to Venice; the by-product, no doubt, of centuries of pollution, absolutely unlike the fresh green-blue of the Adriatic Sea into which they empty. The integral presence of water, part of its urban fabric, is a vital signature of the Venetian image, but the color of the canals, a continuous linear thread contrasting with the colors of streets and facades, is its major component.

A prime feature of urban form, the edge, is ubiquitous in Venice. Beginning with the city, itself an edge—between the sky and the open sea—the formal theme is asserted in the inter-penetration of crenellated buildings with the skyline. Cathedral domes, the Clock Tower, the Campanile in San Marco Square, the sculpted lions of Saint Mark atop the columns of the piazzetta, penetrate the sky from the low-lying plane of the piazza. Piers along the Grand Canal extend the masses of buildings

2-12 Gondola in canal

2-13 Archway

2-14 A back street in Venice

to the sea, and apertures open passages at sea level to permit the entry of gondolas. Colonnades extend building masses into the space of the piazza; sculpted, they replace the building edge with an open system of figure and ground. The perceptual play of forms in Venice is part of its magic.

A glorious amalgam of architecture, sculpture, and painting, Venice is *the* quintessential city of art, as well as the most complete city as a work of art extant. During the height of its Renaissance its great painters—Titian, Veronese, Tintoretto, the Tiepolos—decorated the ceilings and walls of its palaces and churches, and Sansovino its facades; many of these works remain, in situ, as powerful instances of artistic integration. Byzantine mosaics on the interior surfaces of Saint Mark's cathedral show the relationship of color to form—their tesserae shape walls and domes as they narrate the biblical testaments, both old and new. Sensitivity of surface imaging to the volumes of architectonic structure is apparent in these mosaics; the eye of the artisan took the context into account in creating the size and scale of the images.

If these works of art are a daily presence in their city, Venetians in general had to have been profoundly influenced by their impact. Beauty in their surroundings is a common heritage of Venetians; in addition to the gifts of works of stone and imagery, however, is that of the increased capacity to see. Visual sensitivity, in general an Italian attribute, is evident everywhere in the city. All architecture in Venice is colored, and the taste of the Venetian vernacular is at the same time rich and subtle.

2-15 Urban edges: The Piazzetta

In its poor neighborhoods today, when people assemble outdoors in their piazzette, their mellow voices in ordinary conversation resonate richly from wall planes and water surfaces, sounding like dry recitative. Their city is opera and theater, functioning not merely as backdrop or scenery, but as the living tissue itself. At its height Venice was a city of commerce and politics as well as art and, by accounts, as Byzantine in the complexity of its governance, church, society, and trade as its physical shape appears today. It may be the best reminder that a city functions on many more levels than those that are narrowly utilitarian. The city is truly the matrix of civilization.

2-16 Poor neighborhood, Venice

2-17 Urban edges: Cathedral and Piazza San Marco

2-18 Colosseum, Rome

ROME

A characteristic common to all Italian cities is their perceptual clarity. The architectural icons that define their special character provoke immediate recognition—in Rome the Colosseum or the Vatican may be its landmark images. But the geographic context of the city, its seven hills and the spatial meander of the River Tiber determine its shape and influence its major arterials, piazze, and monuments. Eternal Rome, the locus of the ancient empire, stands in the midst of the Baroque city that today identifies it stylistically and, on the whole, predominates as its image.

The urban pattern of Rome is one of open, shapely piazze, connected by arterials proceeding from them, such as that of the ancient Via dei Fori Imperiale from the Piazza del Colosseo, or the Piazza del Corso from the Piazza Venezia—and rather narrow streets. From the vantage point of a piazza, there are a number of options to follow as paths to reach the next large open area. The number and variety of these configurations is further enhanced

2-19 Roman Forum and Trajan column

by the Baroque architecture and fountain and statuary of Rome's master architect and sculptor, Bernini—the Trevi, the Piazza Navona, the Triton. The Spanish Steps, at the edge of the Villa Borghese and its gardens, descend to the Via Condotti—now an active shopping district. The chaos and irritating buzz of engines, the car and motorscooter, have not been banished from the heart of Rome, as they have in Siena and Florence. Though adding confusion to the city experience, they have not erased it. Rome overrun by foreigners—is still Rome, and monumental though its attractions are, they can be visited on foot.

At the heart of the old city, from most landmarks, a major street proceeds; the Roman Forum to the Piazza Venezia, the Piazza Navona to the Corso Vittorio Emanuele, and the Castel Sant'Angelo to the Lungotevere bind this network of large and small spaces. A map belies the perceptual organization of the urban pattern. It looks like an organism, lacking a grid, or the clarifying radial design of a planned city. Rome grew by accrual through two millennia of its history, and monuments overlay and supplant one another—Santa Maria Sopra Minerva, an example, is a Gothic cathedral built on the antique foundations of a temple to Minerva.

2-20 Castel Sant'Angelo

But perceptual clarity depends upon the memorability of places, the visual recall of a Baroque complex, or the kinesthetic experience of traversing the shape of a piazza. On foot, the Piazza Navona, that elongated ellipse, flanked by its Baroque church and disposed by the complex of Bernini's sculpted fountains, remains etched in memory. It is not confused with Michelangelo's Capitoline Hill, because the urban spaces themselves are unique in their placement geographically and by the plan of their configurations. A city designed by artists, architects, and sculptors over two millennia becomes graphically embedded in the totality of human memory by historical features, by visual and tactile experience, and by kinesthetic recall. Once traversed, *seen*, and truly *experienced*, these perceptual images linger and can be retrieved. Orientation takes place even with a fragmentary view of a monument, from a distance, or within the confines of a narrow street.

To the richness and variety of forms—Rome's architecture, sculpture, and urban spaces—is added the special quality of Mediterranean light. Rich and intense, but not harsh, the light of Rome is met by the chromatic sensation of its color. Sunlight reflected from the marble surfaces of the ancient ruins registers

2-21 Piazza Navona

2-22 Bernini fountain, Piazza Navona

2-23 Courtyard in a Roman palazzo

2-24 Santa Maria Sopra Minerva

2-25 Villa Medici

on the retina as intense, but not blinding. Lively and stimulating, the light casts carved surfaces into sharp relief, plays over the muscular forms of Bernini's figures, and creates dark shadows in the marbles' hollows. The umbrella pines of Rome, deep green, standing on its hills against a bright blue sky, are by contrast silhouetted as hovering, playful, dark shapes.

Color enhances the narrow streets throughout the city with saturated, deep, rich brown-reds, burnt siennas, earthy yellows, occasional pinks In the modern suburbs at its perimeter, the hues of the central ancient city are repeated on facades. Roman color is redolent of the Earth, solid and stable, a counterweight to the evanescence of the Meditteranean light.

2-26 Via Condotti, Rome

2-27 Duomo, Florence

2-28 Brunelleschi, Church of Santo Spirito, Florence

FLORENCE

The birthplace of the Italian Renaissance, the Tuscan city of Firenze is at the center of the heart of Italy. Situated in a valley, it is subjected to the conditions of winter and weather, the cold, damp, and fog, which tend to diminish the intensity of ambient light.

Cultivated and refined, Florentine visual qualities express dignity and restraint. Tuscan Italian represents the standard for the Italian language; it is equivalent to Oxford English. The extraordinary intellectual and artistic achievements of the period of the early Renaissance took place within the Florentine context of learning, stimulating the

2-29 Lungarno near Piazza Goldoni, Florence

2-30 Lungarno

2-31 Piazza Goldini

encouragement of the arts and the enlightened patronage of its princely families, particularly the Medici, the Strozzi, Brancacci, and Pazzi.

The architectural achievements of Brunelleschi and Michelangelo; the sculpture of Michelangelo, Donatello, and Ghiberti; the paintings of Giotto, Masaccio, Botticelli, and Leonardo da Vinci are evident in the city's fabric. The great cupola of the Duomo, designed by Brunelleschi, was the outstanding feat of engineering for its time. And from the steps of that same cathedral, the architect drew the first linear construction of the image of the medieval Baptistery opposite, initiating the invention of Perspective.

The Renaissance city prevails today. The proportions of its palazzi are elegant, in scale with one another and their surroundings. Facades are grand, even monumental, but so faithfully designed to human scale that they do not overwhelm or intimidate. Sculpted and painted embellishment is generally understated and in scale with the facades. The standards set by Renaissance architects eventually were disseminated throughout the world, adapted and copied, then reappearing in more pompous versions the further in time and distance they were from the source.

Size, scale, and proportion were Florentine issues that evolved visually and mathematically from within the context of classical humanism—man was the measure of all things. "Divina proporzione," the golden section, derived from the proportions of classical buildings, was applied to Renaissance architecture, and "la bella costruzione," the advent of one-point perspective, was celebrated by painters, sculptors, and architects alike. Fundamentally intellectual, the rigor of these

systems predominated in Renaissance art and architecture and are visible in the city of Florence today.

The urban pattern, dominated by the piazze—Piazza del Duomo, Piazza Santa Croce, Piazza della Signoria—configures the city as a series of open spaces. Between them the streets are closer to grids, more rational than those of Rome or the meanders of Venice.

Clarity and order begin with the setting. The Florentine valley basin is bisected by the River Arno. But at the heart of the city, the river is

2-33 Perceptual city: View of Duomo from the Piazza della Signoria

2-34 Lungarno Amerigo Vespucci

2-35 Ponte Vecchio

relatively straight, and from its banks it offers a free and sweeping view of the whole. The distinctive and beautiful bridges, such as the Ponte Santa Trinitá, restored or reconstructed after bombardment in World War II are parallel paths connecting sectors of the city. The most renown, the Ponte Vecchio, left intact by British warplanes, links the Piazza della Signoria and the Uffizi across the Arno to the Via Guicciardini and the Pitti Palace.

Radial order at the Piazza Goldoni provides the one-point perspectives of the converging Via della Vigna Nuova, Via del Moro, and Via del Parione at the heart of the mercantile sector. The shapes of the cathedral piazze are each uniquely configured; the seat of government, the Piazza della Signoria, open and democratically accessible, is spacious. The Uffizi, government offices before conversion to the museum, is an extended U-shaped, four-storied structure, combining a large, colonnaded portico at ground level with galleries above. From the Piazza della Signoria, a view of the enclosed courtyard terminates at a one-point perspective through a massive arch to the river Arno beyond. Like a secular clois-

ter this space is meditative, despite its monumental size. Perceptual clarity is reinforced in the Florentine city plan by conceptual order.

An emphasis on form is characteristically Florentine; unlike other Italian cities, its streets are sparsely colored. The Duomo, a celebration of surface marbles, is a Gothic display of white, dark green, and pink-purple stone, a multicolored expanse of color and form. In totality the effect of this color structure is patterned and linear. Similarly, the paintings of the Florentine, Botticelli, show a predominance of line and shape over color; he uses color locally, within shapes, to describe or define areas of clothing, or to place or isolate objects from one another in pictorial space.

Along the Arno, however, a gradient of color occurs in the continuum of facades from the Lungarno Amerigo Vespucci toward the Ponte Vecchio. Grand palaces of stone, light

2-36 Lungarno near the Ponte Vecchio

in coloration, gradually increase in intensity and hue on less elegant edifices closer to the Ponte. From neutral and bright to yellow and pink ochers, the facades enliven and change in proximity to the mercantile center. Whether by custom or design, the longest, most visible Florentine street has been orchestrated with color as a temporal sequence.

On the Oltrarno, the opposite bank of the river, and the traditional sector of the working classes—the skilled artisans in leather, wood, and secular and religious artifacts—the buildings are more colorful. Along the riverbank, buildings reconstructed after the Second World War were painted with more saturated versions of yellow and red ocher, as are the streets of the neighborhood beyond. Within the districts of the Oltrarno vernacular expression is less restrained, yet contained within the boundaries of Florentine taste.

2-37 Santo Spirito, facade

2-38 Oltrarno

2-39 Siena, Piazza del Campo

SIENA

Medieval Italian cities were autonomous states, each with its own well-defined character. Siena is situated south of Florence, within three steep hills in the region of Tuscany, and retains the shape of a fortress town. The principal rival of Firenze in the Middle Ages, it eventually fell to Florentine domain.

In plan, the city is a series of curvilinear streets surrounding the immense, sunken, fan-shaped dish of the Piazza del Campo, the site of the Sienese annual ritual battle, the Palio. Large enough to accommodate teams of joisting equestrians, banners, and a huge audience, the campo, in quotidian repose, is vastly open and overscale for the single human figure. Like dots, people traverse its space on their way through town because all surrounding passageways generate from its perimeter. These paths wind, almost swirl spatially, repeating the large arc to the north, while the Palazzo Publico is seated to the south. In sunshine, its great tower casts a moving shadow against the gleaming pattern of brick pavement of the Campo, marking time like a huge sundial.

Siena is a city surrounded by walls, accessible now through its main gates only by foot. Medieval winding streets are tight passageways even for pedestrians, and vehicles, except those for services, are excluded. The

character and quality of these streets are Gothic and darkened because of the height and proximity of the buildings. Tunneled passageways link them to the Campo; often obscure spaces, the tunnels open to the dazzling light reflected in the piazza.

The great Duomo and the Baptistery behind and steeply below it are connected by a marble staircase. A ceremony of entry is enacted in directing the pedestrian's pace, a sequence of footsteps determined by the topography of the hill site. The Duomo is a great Gothic

2-41 Sienese street

2-42 Baptistery and staircase leading to Duomo

wedding cake of white marble; its sculpted figures, embellished niches, interstices, and drainpipes all form the fantastic shape of a crenellated edge against the sky. The bell tower decreases the rate of black and white horizontal slices of the church's sides as it rises high behind it. The striped scheme is repeated in the medieval gate, entry to the piazza. During the 200 years of its construction, the church complex combined the handiwork of forty artists and many more artisans, including those of the Pisani, Ghiberti, and Donatello.

2-43 Sienese Duomo—edge

2-44 Lucca, medieval walls

LUCCA

Situated west of Firenze, Lucca is a medieval fortress town, with its origins at the time of Caesar's Rome. Its ramparts stand, entirely encircling the old city, replete with towers. Relatively small, its main streets are roughly parallel to one another; at intersections some form a 90° axis. Within these quadrants, patterns of smaller streets and piazze prevail as labyrinthian patterns more typical of medieval towns.

On foot the town offers the experience of narrow, stone-paved streets, varied in rhythm by open spaces of piazze. The compression of its narrow pathways contrast with the open generosity of the Piazza del Mercato at the center, or of the Piazza Napoleone, reminders of the significance of street life in urban Italy where people congregate to visit, attend Mass, shop, or merely perambulate. Where the urban pattern of a street is interrupted by a piazzetta before a church or palace, the vista closes.

2-45 Street, Lucca

2-46 Duomo, Lucca

Gothic facades of the Duomo and the church of San Michele are wonderfully inventive examples of medieval artisanship. The sheer variety of carving on the delicate columns of the porticos, some embellished with fine intarsia of colored stones; the gentle Romanesque arches decorated with low relief; and the playful scaling of figures make the marble facades a surprising visual delight. Architecturally, the facade is the main event; heavy with stone and entirely frontal, each church faces its respective piazza, and from the side, the architecture abruptly turns to a lateral plane of unadorned simplicity. Front to side, an expression of vernacular buildings is articulated here with great style.

A regional stone constitutes the building material of the town center. Luminous pink, reddish-brown in color, it appears very heavy, and was meticulously cut, hewn, and fitted in square blocks, in alternating rows, without mortar. In twilight, before eventide, it glows, a low-value vibration to the eye in the midst

of the darkening closure of the narrow street. Unique to Lucca, in daylight its surface radiates reddish light, in its effect, almost fleshy, like an organism.

Painted surfaces in Lucca are terra-cotta, the solid, stable hues of baked earth, used often with chrome green details on shutters and the lintels of apertures. The green/red contrast

2-47 Stone of Lucca

occurs frequently throughout the town. When sunlight prevails, a phenomenon occurring in narrow passageways takes place. Light, reflected from an adjacent surface, will transmit its color by physical scattering. At a luminous moment, a facade, painted a delicate light green is magically intensified in saturation when sunlight, illuminated and reflected from a terra-cotta wall, imbues the narrow space with red. Such experiences may occur randomly, or they may be the result of long association or familiarity with the behavior of light in a given place. It is possible that a visually sensitive people, once observing the event, may playfully assign colors to their environment to elicit or reevoke these magical transformations.

2-48 Facade, Lucca

2-49 Luminous street

2-50 Facade, San Gimignano

SAN GIMIGNANO

The city of towers is a Tuscan hill town, indelible in memory for its unique profile. Situated within a landscape that has been tended for thousands of years by human hands, it appears like an apparition in an extensive garden. Fourteen towers remain of the far more numerous arrangement during the Middle Ages, serving then as battlements.

A city of stone, it presents a neutral field to the eye, nearly uniform, of medium-warm value. On closer examination, the towers appear to have been constructed of a variety of stones and, in some cases, by accrual over time, rebuilt. Some were well hewn, of square, fitted elements; others seem to have been made of composites of rubble. Spongy volcanic stones intersperse with well-wrought marbles. A patina of microorganisms has modified the whole. Apart from the age and variety of stones, and an occasional use of bricks, there is very little applied color. Overall, the environment is sere and medieval.

The Piazza del Duomo and Piazza del Popolo are large spaces, configured at ground plane by the hill, which varies their heights. Stone staircases add a texture to the Piazza del Duomo, affording views of the city streets, which are altered by altitude. A main thoroughfare climbs quite precipitously from

2-51 San Gimignano, street

the piazza. Wider than anticipated for a city of such small size it leads the pedestrian past the urban center.

The urban patterns of medieval Italian towns are varied by the conformations of their hilly sites. In each, the special nature of a particular environment is reflected in the urban shape. Rather than opposing the natural environment, these cities were built to fit within its parameters, resulting in places that are memorable in recall, each one perceptually distinctive.

2-52 Piazza del Duomo, San Gimignamo

2-53 Valdichiana, view from Cortona

CORTONA

Situated at the pinnacle of a hill, Cortona overlooks the vast plane of the valley of Valdichiana. An ancient town, its walls were first built by the Etruscans in the fourth century B.C. and, within its center, an Etruscan museum of significant size displays the art and artifacts of these pre-Roman inhabitants of Tuscany.

A vertiginously steep street connects a portal of city wall with the Piazza della Republica. Service vehicles and selected visitors may approach this path in first gear; others must climb as they walk. The destination is worth the effort. The piazza opens into an urban space with a large civic building that overlooks a lively market center. Climbing

2-54 Piazza della Republica, Cortona

2-55 Street in Cortona

2-56 Neighborhood in Cortona

2-57 Nuanced color in facades, piazza, Cortona

2-58 Urban space in Cortona

immediately behind it, the Piazza Signorelli unfolds, flat, open, and accessible. Narrow streets descend from this plateau, a series of meanders containing ancient stone steps and passageways that curve and open, or dip and lead—all of them unique. Occasionally a glimpse of filtered green landscape appears behind the portal of a passageway. Otherwise, a sense of containment is the spatial experience of this medieval town.

Ambient light is filtered. While in full sunshine the town is luminous, the configurations of buildings and passageways confer closure to the streets; light appears in patches in shadowy contexts. High above the valley, the atmosphere is like a veil, diminishing in intensity as it disperses the Sun's rays.

Although much is built of stone, the ancient stuccoed walls have been layered with paint. Soft, suave, discreet coloration, moving from

butter yellow to apricot impasto, or light salmon to whitened amber, color is light in value as well as in touch. Repainted newly, its intensity is kept to match the old and faded application and to retain harmony with its neighbors. On a brightly sunny day these light but saturated colors bounce from surface to surface in the narrow medieval streets, creating luminous fields. In Cortona blue appears, whitened on a wall or more fully saturated as a doorway, a hue relatively rarely seen in Italy.

Despite its small size, and relative isolation, Cortona is urbane. Its people resemble the painted portrait images of their Etruscan ancestors; some have inherited their enormous, expressive black eyes. Luca Signorelli, a painter of the High Renaissance, was born and worked here; the Diocesan Museum in town contains some of his major works, as do the churches. Finding masterpieces in Tuscan hill towns is a frequent occurrence.

2-59 Piazza Maggiore, Bologna

In the region of Emilia Romagna, Bologna is major northern Italian city. Renowned for its university, founded in 1050 and the first established in Europe, Bologna is a cultivated city with an active civic life. Full of students, its large Piazza Maggiore is the site of assembly for open-air meetings, rallies, and concerts.

An Etruscan city first, it was later Roman, and in the Middle Ages it was an independent city-state. The central city plan is large in scale, and radial in design. From the Piazza di Porta Ravegnana, six streets radiate in a fan shape. The Via del Indipendenza, a broad, main thoroughfare, bisects and terminates the circular, radiating pattern, and initiates a grid. Within these squarish sectors small streets are less regularly arranged. A feature of Bolognese main streets is their broad pedestrian arcades. Crowded with vendors and street life, they achieve formal separation of humanity from motorized vehicles, unique for modern Italy.

The urbanity of Bologna is physically reinforced by broad vistas and the generous proportions of its thoroughfares. The Palazzo Comunale, and other civic buildings are large in scale, as is the Basilica di San Petronio. More secular and civic in urban character, more northern, Bologna conveys the spirit of active, contemporary life. Its historic past, its monuments and architecture, seem to weigh less heavily or exert less influence on the present than those of other Italian cities.

2-60 Urban space—arcade in Bologna

2-61 View of Jerusalem

JERUSALEM, ISRAEL

Jerusalem rises out of the Judean desert, an apparition in light against the pink/yellow hills of Moab. Seen from a distance, the golden Dome of the Rock dominates the topography of the city. The Temple Mount stabilizes the entire structure of the Old City, providing a horizontal plane, clearly visible from afar. The gold leaf of the dome's surface glitters in the abundant sunshine, and under all atmospheric circumstances remains a focus, isolated against the sky and hills.

A city bathed in light, the harsh reflected light of the surrounding desert blanches out color, but reveals the reticulation and textures of stone. The mystery of light as color is contained in these stones, which from its ancient origins in time were used to build this city. The buttery-colored stone is slightly translucent, and it reflects golden amber, neutral or rose-violet hues, depending upon the time of day or the angle of incidence of sunlight. At times Jerusalem seems suspended, a mirage. From a distance the urban field is uniform in appearance; buildings, low lying and clustered into a horizontal plane, nearly merge with the environment and integrate with the hills beyond.

2-62 Old City, Jerusalem

The antiquity of the cities of Israel, and the number of cultures that have inhabited them are so complex that it is the archaeologist or historian's task to interpret the markings or remains of their presence. Canaanite, Assyrian, Hittite, Hebrew, Greek, Ptolemaic, Seleucid, Phoenician, Roman, Parthian, Persian, Byzantine, Arab, Crusader, Saracen, Kurd, and Mameluke civilizations all claimed and left their traces in the early history of the land, in addition to the modern Israeli and Arab inhabitants.

In Jerusalem the ancient remains of Herod's wall, sacred to the Jews as the remainder of the second Temple, and the Dome of the Rock on the Temple Mount, sacred to Moslems are located in the heart of the Old City, and the Basilica of the Holy Sepulchre, the most venerated in Christendom, are all contained within the ancient walls. That these major world religions would find in "the city of peace" their sites of holiness, is due in large part, I think, to the physical circumstance of austere barren landscape and intense luminosity of atmosphere. The deep blue of the sky, the clarity and intensity of light, the magical shifting of the colors of the Moab Hills, from warm rose to violet to cool neutral, must have appeared as visions in ancient times, as they can seem hallucinatory now.

The unity of effect of the walled city and its immediate surroundings is due to the small scale of the buildings, which permits the Temple Mount to float and dominate the complex, and the color of the stone used in their construction. The inevitable sprawl of the modern high-rise habitations developing on the surrounding hills is mitigated only somewhat by the continued use of these materials, varieties of Kenoman limestone, the golden-red Mizi Achmar and cream-colored Mizi Yahudi.

The Old City is walled and approached through its ancient gates; Suleiman's Damascus gate, Jaffa Gate, and Zion Gate, among eight entrances to the city, surround the Jewish, Christian, Moslem, and Armenian quarters. Labyrinthian passageways define the streets and enclosures; some as small as closets are densely occupied. Crowded with shouks (markets), mosques, people, donkeys, it is as if time had stopped and one were experiencing the ancient past. Buildings have been constructed on top of rooftops, an accrual of urban densities; here an African tribe dwells in the midst of the Old City.

In the Arab quarter the walls are whitewashed; and surrounding the entrances of houses, symbols of Mecca are painted. Other apertures are designated by borders of blue— a mystical color—left unevenly painted from the doorway's edge. The Dome of the Rock itself, glittering in gold leaf, is supported by walls surfaced with Persian tiles, predominantly blue, a reference to the sky.

Arcaded streets, covered by archways or temporary awnings, are a feature of Middle Eastern cities; they shield passageways from the Sun's intensity. Some, built on steep hills, contain broad steps, suited to both human

and animal footpace; they exclude vehicles. The light here, scattered by the proximity of buildings to one another, produces a filtered ambience. The facade of a building appears ocher in the light, and above, and to the distance shows incremental changes in its intensity to a gentle, buttery yellow. In contrast, on an adjacent street in the Old City, its stone facades in shadow appear violet. This complementary color relationship is the consequence of light and shadow on stone surfaces, in the intensely luminous field of the city's site.

2-65 Jerusalem, street in shadow

2-66 Jerusalem, street in light

2-67 Jericho from Masada

JERICHO AND THE SINAI

Jericho, 820 feet below sea level, is one of
the oldest cities on earth, an oasis in the
desert. Nearby are the remains of Qumran,
the habitat of the Essenes, the sect of Jesus
and the place where the Dead Sea Scrolls
were found. The Dead Sea, with a median
depth of 1300 feet below sea level, the lowest
point on earth, has a concentrated accumula-
tion of mineral salts, making it ten times
denser than ordinary seawater. Ancient
Egyptians imported bitumin extracted
from it for embalming their dead. Near
its shores is the rock of Masada.

The antiquity of the land is visible in the
stone remains of civilizations. The stones of
the Sinai are purple, those of the Dead Sea
are indigo and ocher, and the rocks of Eilat
at the shore of the Red Sea are yellow. Bitten
by light, the rocks of the Sinai crumble in
the hand.

2-68 Santa Caterina Monestery, Sinai

3-1 View of Guadalajara

REGIONS OF LIGHT

The spatial sense of Mexican cities and towns varies by location within the rugged geography of its terrains. The great range of the Sierra Madre Mountains extends like a spine throughout the north/south axis of the continent. Effectively dividing the country into its distinct regions, these vary greatly, a consequence of the the complexity of prevailing geologic conditions.

A semiarid desert prevails in the north, an effective barrier to the U.S. borders; lush coastal vegetation abounds on the subtropical west coast; the high plateau country of the capital, Mexico, Districto Federal, is the most inhabited; and to the south, separated by steep mountain passes, the valley of Oaxaca presents a second region of mesa. To the east, mountains descend to the wet coastal plain of the Gulf states and the peninsula of Yucatán. Active volcanos, Popocatépetl and Ixtaccíchuatl ring Mexico City and Puebla, a colonial city to its south. Consequently, the configurations of the cities of Mexico are in part determined by geography, whether extended expansively on the relatively flat terrain of mesas, as in Mexico, D.F., or Oaxaca, or clinging tenaciously to mountainous slopes, as does San Cristobal de las Casas in Chiapas.

On the site of the Aztec city, Tenochtitlán, the central district of the modern city, Mexico, D.F., was constructed, and in the great square area of the Zócalo its ancient perimeters can be traced. Aztec Tenochtitlán was built on an island in a lake, its central area was laid out with geometric precision, and the streets and causeways were wide and straight—placed at 90° angles to its perimeters. The area contained teocali, or temples built on steep pyramidal bases, to the Aztec god of rain, Tláloc, and that of war, Huítzilopochtli, in addition to the palace of the ruler, Móctezuma. The ancient city contained floating gardens and a zoo, and according to the accounts of its Spanish conquerors was finely built and resplendent. Ruined by the conquistadors and plundered, this once-glittering city was rebuilt by Cortés as Mexico City, on the original site. In the sixteenth century the plaza mayor, or Zócalo, was the largest in the world, larger than the Piazza di San Marco in Venice.

3-2 Dawn, Mexico, D.F.

Many of the churches built after the conquest in the sixteenth century throughout Mexico contained large, open-air chapels, a colonial architectural form designed specifically to gather together novice native congregants for their conversion to Catholicism. Some of these spaces could accommodate up to 20,000 people in their atrios, or open courts. Their scale was not unfamiliar to the natives. Pre-Aztec civilization had constructed the monumental, precisely aligned city of pyramids at Teotihuacán, possibly as an astronomical observatory. At Monte Albán the Zapotecans of Oaxaca had erected a complex of pyramids to the Sun.

The Mayan civilization produced cities in the Yucatán, Uxmal, Chichén Itzá, and Tulúm, and Palenque in the rain forest of Chiapas. These consisted of elaborate architectural monuments, embellished with sculpture and polychromed, carved reliefs. Within were chambers containing wall paintings and ceramic ceremonial vessels painted with narrative imagery. A highly developed and sophisticated culture, Mayan archaeologic remains reveal a unique picture language, a numeric system, and calendars of great accuracy predicting the time and frequency of solar eclipses. Mayan ceramic sculptures rival in refinement those of ancient Greece.

3-3 San Francisco Acatepéc, Mexico

Although most of the population of the country today is mestizo, the mix of Spaniards with indigenous people, in Oaxaca and Chiapas, the two southernmost states, dwell the original inhabitants. Cortés and his horsemen found traversing the Sierra Madre del Sur a daunting prospect and stopped their conquest of Mexico before Oaxaca. Hence, to the south Zapotecan (Oaxaca), Lacandón (Chiapas), and Mayan populations (Yucatán) remain intact.

The ancient civilizations of Mesoamerica remain in ruins, but the people, their spoken languages, chiefly Náhuatl, and some of their rituals have survived in small villages and towns. While the great artistic traditions may

have vanished, the exuberant spirit that created them exists today in the folk arts and crafts throughout Mexico. Region by region, village cultures produce ceramics, the black pottery of Coyotepéc in the valley of Oaxaca, weavings and textiles, the tiles of Puebla, the candelabras and ceramic sculptures of Acatlán, tinwork, and the artifacts of silversmiths of Taxco. Many local traditions and creativity in everyday artistry like the baked figurines for the Day of the Dead in Oaxaca are alive and thriving. Included in this artistic spirit is the tradition of coloring their cities.

The presence of Nature is felt in Mexican towns where, in the intense sunlight, the brilliant reds, magentas, oranges, and pinks of bougainvilleas may be juxtaposed with the llamarada blossoms of yellow-orange. Crotons grow to the size of trees, with leaves streaked green, yellow, and red that reach a meter in length. Contrasts are dramatic. In the rainy season torrential downpours will take place on one side of the street, while the sun may shine brightly on the other. In Mexico, D.F., dawn is a spectacular visual drama. Recorded minute by minute, the spectral array of hues shift from indigo to cerulean blue to purple to flame to gold, a gorgeous overload of visual sensation.

The ceiling of the church of San Francisco in Acatepéc, near Puebla, one of the earliest built after the conquest, represents the overlay of Spain on the native culture—a veneer. Carved by Indian artisans, the profusion of angels, gilded clouds, and the holy spirit, images of Catholicism, were gessoed, painted, and gold leafed in a style more Indian than Christian. The encrustation of colors and forms totally cover the barrel vault and dome. Daylight, skimming the surfaces, reveals their rich complexity and the total effect is not unlike the pyrotechnic display of the sky at dawn.

3-4 Santa Clara, New Mexico

SANTA FE, NEW MEXICO

The town of Santa Fe, and the settlements surrounding it, represent an amalgam of Native American cultures and the colonization of the area, first by the Spanish, then by the United States. The region includes Santa Fe, now a sophisticated cultural center, which preserves the architectural style of the American Southwest, Taos, and the reservations of the aboriginal Navajo tribes in nearby Pueblo.

These inhabited areas are subsumed by a landscape of vast grandeur. At an altitude of

Cristo appear as floating violet masses below a deeply saturated, serene blue sky. The sky dominates, filled with low-lying bands of huge cumulus clouds which hover and move majestically. Below, semiarid, the earth contrasts in hue. Soft clay colors, reddish browns, pinks, sand, ochers change to deep purple in shadow. High altitude produces a lucent clarity, rather than the harshness associated with desert light. Indeed, the environment represents "The Land of Enchantment," a legend that the state's auto license plates appropriate, proudly—but ironically—declare.

3-5 Pueblo, Taos, New Mexico

3-6 Hotel, Santa Fe

6950 feet, Santa Fe was settled on a high plateau, the site of choice of the aboriginal tribes of the Navajo, Santa Clara, and Puye—now reservations. In this area Nature reigns. The atmosphere remains exceptionally clear, a consequence of low population density and no industry. Ambient light and distant swaths of great, horizontal planes of mesa produce colors of translucency, magical in effect. Mountain ranges of the distant Sangre de

Pueblo, the Navajo reservation near Taos, despite its small size, is an urban complex, a consolidation of multiple small units, several storeys in height, with access to its chambers through doors, or roofline apertures—an urban form, reflecting the community of its tribal inhabitants. Soft, dense forms of kivas and outdoor ovens stand independently in open spaces, many covered by a network of wooden supports to provide shade. A byplay

3-7 Pueblo, detail

an economy of means and use of nature, simplicity, and completeness in the dwelling place of a people, set harmonically into the context of the landscape.

In the town of Santa Fe, contemporary Americans have preserved some of these qualities, borrowing the adobe style to build simulated structures that exceed in height the structural capacity of baked clay. Surface colors are carefully chosen to mimic it. The byplay of regional light adds violet to clay color on an adobe wall in shadow. The distinction between the authentic and fake is kept to a minimum. The vernacular style is essentially simple and small in scale. Wooden porches, columns, doors, and the frames of apertures are painted sky blues, malachite greens, aquas—hues lighter in value than the contrasting earth colors of walls.

3-8 Street in Santa Fe

of lights and shadows, these add sharp patterns to contrast with the integrated form and color of the surrounding adobe structures, and earth. The syntax of the Pueblo is at once more complex, and more integrated than that of the town of Santa Fe. Tightly clustered spaces, structurally interdependent, provide places for dwelling, preparing food, and other life-sustaining activities, as well as religious rituals. Pueblo represents a fragment of the survival of the Navajo; it reflects in its built form their spirit and values,

If these adaptions of the local vernacular may be self-conscious, the ambience of Santa Fe is generally harmonic within its surroundings, reflective of its native origins, and respectful of the natural environment.

3-9 Simon Rodia: Watts Tower, Los Angeles

LOS ANGELES

Known as the "New City," Los Angeles was one of the first established in America. The original Spanish settlement, "Nuestra Senora de la Ciudad de Los Angeles," remains marked today by a tiny plaza opposite Union Station downtown, adjacent to a tourist replica of an open Mexican street market.

Absent a coherent form, the city extends to the limits of its natural boundaries and beyond; the San Gabriel Mountains to the north, Pacific Ocean to the west and south, and Mojave Desert to the east. Even these have been transcended by development in the San Fernando Valley since World War II, and at the present time increasingly eastward to Bakersfield. The capacities of existing freeways, consequently, have become stressed to gridlock. Overall the city image is one of massive sprawl, the consequence of the development of *individual* dwellings without regard to the shaping of districts or centers. Neighborhoods do exist; the older city of Pasadena maintains civic character, as does Beverly Hills. Santa Monica, planned initially with wide streets and ample setbacks of its low-lying bungalows, is visually distinctive. More recently, Venice Beach and Culver City have undergone extensive urban development, clarifying and making distinct their city images.

Districts are difficult to distinguish because their boundaries are visually incoherent; only repeated experience eventually orients the individual. Some, like Beverly Hills, were given urban character when founded, which was further reinforced in the 1980s by the development of the City Center designed by Charles Moore. Frank Gehry's Santa Monica Mall complex, a huge graphic sign, orients one; it tends to function visually as a self-contained landmark, however, rather than being integrated into the total environment. On the whole, Wilshire Boulevard, a major artery, is also distinguished more by its individual landmarks, such as the Los Angeles County Museum and La Brea tarpits, than by urban patterns, districts, or plazas. MacArthur Park downtown and the old Wilshire shopping district do contain Art Deco buildings, and refer to historic moments in the city's past. Elsewhere buildings are undistinguished high rises, absent any visual character to engender nostalgic associations or connection with the environment; they are places to get through on the way to someplace else at the greatest possible speed.

What distinguishes the region/city is its domestic architecture. Barnsdall was designed by Frank Lloyd Wright. The Greene and Greene Bros. in Pasadena, influenced by Japanese house design and the Craftsmen's movement, created totally integrated designs of architecture, interiors, furniture, and fixtures of wood. They set a pattern for the vernacular California bungalow. The Modernists R. M. Schindler and Richard Neutra designed houses that integrated the natural surroundings with built structures;

their signature open plans and flowing spaces became one of modern architecture's hallmarks. Irving Gill, influenced by mission architecture and the adobe style developed houses with arcades and passageways connected to gardens. Clearly, the beauty of natural surroundings and the benignity of the climate was a presence felt and responded to in the works of these architects.

Individual expression is the essential quality of more recent architecture. Frank Gehry created a formal vocabulary of the fragmentation aesthetic in Los Angeles, a metaphor of the city and of the times. Chain-link fencing, a democratic statement, is also a comment on the ordinary industrial landscape, the utilitarian surface.

"The City of Angels"—once a paradise—*is* so in pockets, in the canyons and mountain passes, along the beach at Malibu, and in large scale on the Palos Verdes Peninsula, where overall the landscape design of Frederick Law Olmsted prevails. Here development was shaped and controlled, resulting in a unique combination of domestic dwellings in relationship to the natural context. In the gilded (and guarded) neighborhoods of Bel-Air, Brentwood, and Beverly Hills, the urban patterns are circuitous, and landscape designs isolate and define an individual's domain, offering the sense of privacy and remove from the society of "flat-land." America's romantic aspirations, that of the lone individual in relation to a vanishing frontier are played out here. On rare clear days, after a Santa Ana wind has driven the pollution out of the basin, the air is pellucid, as it must have been when the early Spanish settlers first discovered and named the site.

The light is complex. Essentially that of a desert, it is harshly bright, flattening building surfaces until they appear as cardboard backdrops. A nearly shadowless environment, the Sun is almost perpendicular to the Earth at noon in midsummer, allowing maximum reflectivity. The atmosphere is influenced by geography. Mountain ranges create a basin of the vast area, and ocean air, cooler than the desert's, is trapped beneath its heat, causing a thermal inversion. The layer of air beneath this is very stable, causing a visible clarity—now only in the absence of smog. One wonders, if the internal combustion engine had not radically altered it, whether the central image/metaphor of this city might not have remained the province of angels!

To support the metaphor, color, induced by material structures that permit the indirect reflection of light, as cellular structures do naturally, would greatly enhance the built environment. The intense reflectivity of desert light, in the environmental context of the Los Angeles basin, permits the use of color in the urban pattern to a far greater extent than now obtains. In this brilliant environment, paradoxically, color is eschewed; for the most part choices for exterior surfaces of houses are beiges, tans, neutrals, or pastels, pallid and timid responses to the bright effusion of regional light.

3-10 Caribbean sunset

THE CARIBBEAN

The islands of this region, the Greater Antilles, Cuba, the Dominican Republic, and Puerto Rico, were colonized by Spain; those of the Lesser Antilles, the group of Leeward and Windward Islands, were once French and British. Under discussion here are the islands of British Barbados, Trinidad, and the tiny island of Vieques, off the coast of Puerto Rico.

Barbados is situated near the Equator at latitude 13° to the north, and longitude 60°. This region is located in proximity to the origin of the global weather system. As the Equator heat rises, causing cold air from the North and South Poles to move; this massive pattern, like water boiling from the bottom of a pot, creates the convection of large-scale motions of the atmosphere. At the same time, light reflectivity is at its maximum at the Equator, visible as instability in the atmospheric effects at sunset, and the ever-changing colors of ocean volume.

These physical facts cause psychological effects, better illustrated than described. However, the volume color of the sea fluctuates rapidly, registering on the human eye rather than the camera. From moment to moment the Caribbean changes; at first it

3-11 Fishing boat, Barbados

appears turquoise, then blue-violet—under clouds, becoming gray-green, it shifts to blue-green, all within a period of seconds. Light affects the crystal clarity of the total volume of water, and not merely its surface.

From a small plane I photographed the sky at sunset, an event that lasts about 45 minutes. Overall, a red-violet/yellow-gold polarity between atmosphere and clouds was the physical effect. Rose-pinks, orange-pinks, mauves, light yellows ascending to cream whites in clouds—aloft and suspended in the luminous sky—contrasted with the atmosphere's colors, from light

green-tinged yellow to deeper violet in its descent to darkness. Despite the range of hues, and their near-complementary relationships, delicacy is Nature's aesthetic here, distinct from the pyrotechnical drama of a Mexican sunrise. Color complexity may be the result of the instability of the light. Nature's displays have not gone without notice by the native population.

In Bridgetown, Barbados, the blues of sky and sea are repeated in the facades of buildings and the boats of fishermen. Contrasting details are small and restrained; a turquoise boat has a cadmium yellow stripe painted

3-12 Bridgetown

along its side for visibility at sea. Windows and doorways are delineated with white or dark boundaries. The facade of a store is divided by color, its upper storey painted a cool, creamy blue changes with almost imperceptible subtlety to a greener blue of equal value, below. On a street in Bridgetown a light and delicate pink is used on a building. Unlike the exuberant, full-throated colors of Mexico, those of Barbados can be subtle and restrained.

At Trinidad houses are influenced by the colonial style of India. Front porches with large, overhanging eaves embellish the facades, and ironwork adorns windows. Their colors are similar to those found on Barbados. Where the British colonial influence remains, restraint in coloration is characteristic. Another legacy is literacy; 90 percent of Barbados' population can read and write.

4-1 Paris, urban space

URBAN SPACES

MEDIAN CITIES

PARIS

The "City of Light," the grande dame of cities, Paris owes its image more to the configuration of its plan and streets than to its location. At latitude 48°, it is a mere 7° south of Copenhagen, and only 3° south of London. Yet its visual character differs markedly from these two cities. The lightness and openness of its plazas, the width and ample dimensions of its boulevards, and the grand, but limited, heights of its buildings permit light to enter and broadly play its magic upon forms throughout.

Haussmann's plan for Paris prevails in the central city; it permitted great vistas, monumental, yet humane in scale. The boulevards are generously proportioned, providing grand processionals for the foot and the eye. Ceremonial archways such as the Arc de Triomphe, placed at the radiating convergent points of the intersections of major boulevards, are visually accessible from many directions. These points of orientation provide variety and clarity to the conceptual plan of Paris. Monumental in scale, they do not dwarf the individual, but they do *place* one. Formality and ceremony are the visual messages conveyed. Buildings are massive but, at the height of four stories, they maintain consistency in the city's districts. Heavy in volume, the first storeys of large mansions are proportioned higher than the rest, often with an abbreviated fourth storey under the roofline. This tends to ground each building solidly, structurally, and visually on its foundation, and confer a sense of substance to the architecture. In rows of connected houses, the limitations of heights maintain consistency and harmony. Variety is relegated to the rooftops, where playful chimney pots and rooftop configurations display their shapes. This urban edge is clearly visible across the Seine when its Right Bank is viewed from its Left.

The presence of the Seine, a meander pattern bisecting the city, provides open vistas at its very heart. The Cathedral of Notre Dame, situated on the Ile de la Cité is clearly visible— dominant as a landmark, accessible, and a focal point of orientation. Monet's series of paintings of the cathedral's facade imbued with light and color change entirely in palette. Morning's view is blue and violet, hazy with diffuse light, with little articulation of form. The raking light of late afternoon elicits the sculptural volumes of the great portals and towers, rendered in the warm ochers, reds of long wavelength. Here the building's surface exists as a plane for the byplay of light; otherwise, to the painter it is nonmaterial.

Other major landmarks, the Eiffel Tower and the Louvre are also located near the river, its embankments defining the parameters of essential features of the city. The older districts of Paris are readily located and defined by boundaries that are visually and conceptually clear. On the Left Bank is the district of art galleries, antique shops, and bookstores, and in Montmarte, at one time the location of Picasso's and the Impressionists' studios, the streets are more intimate and inviting to the pedestrian. The mixed use of shops, markets, and apartments is characteristic of the city; everywhere it is vibrant and full of life.

Color prevails on the facades of streets as a delimiting marker of individual buildings adjoined in rows. These will be described in Chapter 6, "City Streets," which compares those of different cities. Generally Parisian color gestalt is one of sophisticated neutrals, relatively high in value on the Munsell scale. This range of colors makes a significant contribution to the image of Paris as a city of light.

4-2 Right Bank of the Seine

4-3 Alpine cemetery

VILLAGE IN THE FRENCH ALPS

A small village in the French Alps, exceptionally clear and distinctive, if anonymous, caught my eye. The light at this altitude is intense and highly reflective. Boundaries of the series of mountain ranges visible from this vantage point were sharp throughout a layered overlapping sequence. Distances would have been difficult to estimate. As far as the eye could see there were crisp edges in the cold air.

In a cemetery nearby, marble stones and ironwork tracery marked the gravesites. Within the luminous shadows, the grayish marble

read as violet. The clarity and delicacy of ironwork delineated arabesques of wreathes, crucifixes, wire bowers. Tiny flowers embellished the stone, adding to the delicacy of scale and feeling.

These visual attributes are clearly related to Swiss sensibility in graphic design. Linearity, a sense of scale, elegance and clarity, simplicity and directness, and an economy of means are its hallmarks. The designer's art, combining these elements of form, may be a visual response to the influence of these qualities in the vernacular and in the essential qualities of the natural environment.

4·4 SoHo, Manhattan

To describe the urban pattern of Manhattan, ascribed by New Yorkers as *New York,* is comparatively direct. Conceptually it is the clearest of cities, a function of its compactness and the orientation and regularity of its grid system. Avenues are extended thoroughfares running north/south; numbered streets are oriented east/west. Fifth Avenue defines the boundary bisecting the design; addresses begin here and increase in number east and westward, greatly facilitating the location of a destination. The distinction made between downtown, midtown, and uptown further clarifies urban spaces; below 14th Street is designated as downtown, the area between this major cross street and 59th Street defines midtown, and uptown continues to the north. In Manhattan's oldest districts below the East Village, streets are designated by name, and, with the decreasing width of the island near City Hall and Wall Street, the grid becomes less distinct.

With usage and by association, the place names of Manhattan add metaphoric intensity to the city's images. Wall Street, the world's economic engine; Mott Street, the destination of immigrants; St. Marks, the East Village bohemia; SoHo, the center of art galleries and, increasingly, of corporate chains that trade on that association, allow instantaneous recognition. Avenues also have their spatial and social distinctions. Park Avenue, once a grand vista, wider than its neighboring parallel pathways and landscaped midlength, has been visually blocked at Grand Central Station—a vehicular midtown passageway—by the high rise of the Met-Life building. Madison Avenue, smaller in scale than Park Avenue, is defined by its elegant boutiques, galleries, and museums. Fifth Avenue, once more elegant, is changing as venerable department stores such as B. Altman, which once catered to a larger middle

class than presently exists, go out of business. The intersection of 57th Street and Fifth Avenue retains Tiffany's and Bendel's, and a block south is the edge of Rockefeller Center; further north, at 59th Street, is the Plaza Hotel—active monuments to the city's history.

Residential neighborhoods throughout the city maintain their existence, despite the changes in population that occur over time. The Lower East Side remains home to immigrant groups, Southern Italians live in "Little Italy," and the Chinese still inhabit "Chinatown"; but Jewish populations of the nineteenth century have been replaced by Puerto Ricans, Koreans, and other Asian groups, as the city absorbed the influx of new citizens. In these ethnic neighborhoods can be found color—imported with their inhabitants from their countries of origin—with mixed results.

These are all functioning, living urban places. In New York once a building ceased to be useful, it was torn down, and another built in its place. This action taken on the once-grand and beautiful Pennsylvania Station at 34th Street was one of barbarism. Not only was a piece of city history destroyed—the gateway and destination by rail to the then world's largest city—but its function has never been adequately redefined. Architecturally Penn Station today is like an oversized bus station in a third-world city. Hopefully, the recently proposed inclusion of the U.S. Post Office on Eighth Avenue will restore a sense of grandeur to the complex.

The image of New York is one of progressiveness, and massive and extended growth. Since the publication of urban critiques, such as Jane Jacob's *The Death and Life of Great American Cities,* and the establishment of organizations for historic preservation and restoration, the philosophy of "tear them down and build them up again" has been challenged. The

4-5 Midtown facade

recent restoration of Grand Central Station is a notable example; having been carefully renovated, it has revitalized the great interior space as an active, indoor urban piazza. But Manhattan continues to be overbuilt, with destructive consequences to the city's functioning and to its appearance.

Globally, its location is latitude 41°, longitude 73 ½°. Its categorization as a median city is defined largely by the quality of light experienced by an observer and its relative position on the Earth's surface. Here the dominance of the built environment is overarching. The configuration of buildings, rising high over the conceptual grid crowds the streets with walls. In the 1920s the creation of the trademark pinnacles on New York skyscrapers was the consequence of zoning laws which once limited the height of buildings. Setbacks were designed to permit light to penetrate the mass of edifices and to control the influence of shadows. Light, reflected from the Atlantic Ocean, the East River, and the Hudson, surrounding the island, seems to bounce and scatter continuously from these surfaces. The visual experience created by this softening and diffusion of light is that of filtering within an urban forest. At street level shade often prevails, causing an overall, even neutrality to the environment. In the 1940s, when the city was less dense, the Dutch painter Mondrian remarked that the light of Manhattan reminded him of Holland's. His comparison may have had something to do with the ubiquitous presence of water, and the distinctive configuration of a landscape that is entirely constructed, features of both urban environments.

The absence of color is characteristic of Manhattan. Expanses of building surfaces are neutral, usually warm, light, ocher-beige. Concrete, the color of stone, and glass, to reflect the surroundings, predominate as material surfaces on skyscrapers. Occasionally, brick apartment buildings break the uniformity. Nonassertive, these surfaces blend and conform to one another, forming continuous passageways on streets as urban backdrops. As diffused light conforms to soft color, angular edges are blurred, decreasing the sense of massive volume which the buildings represent. The color sensorium is relegated to the function of graphic display. Shop windows, signage, directional traffic signals contain color. As brighter areas in their overall neutral surroundings, they draw the eye's attention, for commercial purposes or to direct the flow of vehicles and pedestrians. The prevailing atmosphere, that of utilitarian function and anonymity, is its urbane expression.

Civic places, however, are distinctive in architectonic *form*. The Metropolitan Museum of Art; the main branch of the New York Public Library on Fifth Avenue, its interior recently restored; Wright's Guggenheim Museum; the Whitney, the Frick, and the Cooper-Hewitt Museums; the Museum of Natural History on the west side; downtown City Hall; midtown Grand Central Station—most are the architectural legacy of the nineteenth century. Gramercy Park and Washington Square, as well as smaller urban parks and places, open the tight urban grid to light and air. The great swath of Olmsted and Vaux's Central Park defining the boundary of uptown broadly interrupts Manhattan's grid with artificially created mounds, roads, kiosks, and bridges. It provides the relief of green vegetation and the evidence of nature's seasonal presence in the heart of the great metropolis. And it presents a setting for the rhythm of the skyline surrounding it, a monumental integration of built and natural form, and the unique signature of Manhattan.

BOSTON, MASSACHUSETTS

The "Athens of America," Boston retains much of its eighteenth- and nineteenth-century character and flavor. With one-half million inhabitants as distinct from New York's eight million, the scale is smaller and, consequently, the city itself is more intimate.

The urban pattern is irregular, reflecting the city's origins in the seventeenth century, with its streets radiating from the "hub" as a series of cowpaths. The islands in Massachusetts Bay which were filled in and conjoined included the Back Bay, a great nineteenth-century development. At that time individual building plots were filled at the rapid rate of one per day, and the architecturally distinctive district, consisting entirely of large town houses and mansions, remains intact today. Commonwealth Avenue is a grand, wide processional, landscaped throughout its length, and culminating in the Boston Garden and the Common at the foot of Beacon Hill. It was designed to imitate the Parisian urban pattern of Haussmann's Paris, but the character of domesticity of its architecture is more like that of London's. Despite the wealth and social position of Boston's aristocrats, the architectural character of the Back Bay mansions was kept to scale; a double plot may have been permissible, but the building's heights were kept democratically aligned.

Beacon Street extends throughout the city and forms the southern edge of Beacon Hill. Commonwealth Avenue and Marlborough and Newbury Streets are parallel to it, and form a grid, with cross streets named in alphabetical order. Boylston Street aligns the neighborhood's edge to the business district, a boundary also of Copley Square, Boston's oldest principal urban square. Copley Square is a

landmark, and Back Bay, in close proximity, is one of the most coherent districts in the city and Boston's most distinctive neighborhood. Olmsted's "Emerald Necklace" links the Charlesgate to the Fens to the Muddy River Park to Jamaica Pond, westward 5 miles and beyond into the exurbs. This natural meander integrates city form with its country context, but it is a less distinct edge than that provided by the Charles River. Effectively dividing Boston and Brookline from Cambridge and Charlestown, the Charles is reminiscent of the Thames, but smaller in scale.

As a functioning urban pattern, Boston's is hampered by an antiquated public transportation system—the oldest in the United States—and roads that were not designed for heavy vehicular traffic. It remains to be seen what the impact of the massive highway project, "The Big Dig," will be on the city when completed.

Domestic architecture is a hallmark of the Back Bay, South End, adjacent Brookline, and other distinctive neighborhoods, now prime examples of the pedestrian city, limited in size and scaled to human dimensions. Here building heights were regulated by zoning not to exceed five storeys, and rows of town houses are unified by the use of varieties of red brick and brownstone. Distinction in detailing, entryways, porticos, and rooflines create individual character to dwellings, but the overall integrity of these neighborhoods is strictly maintained.

Democracy prevails in large and small scale in Massachusetts. The location of the State House on Beacon Hill and the integration of public and private domains in that distinctive neighborhood visibly bring the government into physical proximity. Active citizen participation in local government and in the town

meetings of Boston's suburbs keeps politics alive and local. The preponderance of institutions of higher learning, such as Harvard and the Massachusetts Institute of Technology, is reflected in a largely educated population.

Industrial Boston, located at the waterfront at Fort Point Channel, produced an architectural style that was well integrated with the scale and proportion of the domestic city in the nineteenth century. Despite its original function as a manufacturing district, it is visually distinctive and is presently developed as a locale of museums, galleries, and artist's and artisan's studios. Buildings six to eight storeys high, constructed of red or yellow brick, connected in rows, form a district that is human in scale, limited in size, and part of the texture of the city.

Boston's color derives from the use of its building material; varieties of red brick predominate. It was used as street pavement on Beacon Hill and the North End, its oldest neighborhoods, as well as on the surfaces of town houses in the eighteenth and nineteenth centuries. Varieties of warm, darkish red, the bricks confer a sense of sobriety and solidity, but as a domestic material its warmth contributes to the sense of humanity that characterizes the city. Churches were constructed of pudding stone, a conglomerate of materials, a mixed neutral in color. Granite was used throughout the nineteenth century for columns, supporting lintels, and foundation walls. Red sandstone appeared in use in the mid-nineteenth century in the "brownstone" of bow-front town houses, but it proved to be fragile, deteriorating in the New England climate.

4-7 Fort Point Channel, Boston

The piers, with their wharves have been converted into upscale dwellings since the rede-
velopment of the waterfront in the 1960s.
The Quincy Market, designed by Benjamin
Thompson and Associates and developed by
the Rouse Company was one of the earliest
and most successful urban projects of the
time, and it rehabilitated the central market
as a tourist attraction. Adjacent to it, the historic Faneuil Hall and City Center complex
has been revived, and where urban blight
once prevailed in Scollay Square an active
downtown business district now thrives.
From the banks of the Charles River, on the
Cambridge side, the view of Boston's Beacon
Hill and Back Bay can be seen in its entirety.
The State House's golden dome is a dominant
landmark on the hill's configuration,
functioning as a nodal point. The eighteenth-
century configuration of rows of town houses

4-8 Back Bay, Boston

of uniform height form horizontal bands of
dark red against the mass of towering gray
edifices of the late twentieth-century city.
Two separate urban patterns overlap to
occupy the city's site and form its visual
image from this vantage point.

CITIES IN SHADOW

LONDON

At latitude 51°, longitude 0°, location itself does not account for London's designation as a city in shadow. Rather, the climate, producing its characteristic precipitation and fog, lowers the intensity of sunlight on average and creates the image.

The capital city of an empire that once extended to the American, Indian, and Australian continents, London bears the symbols of a great world power. At the pinnacle of hierarchy reigned a monarchy, now of course, primarily symbolical. Images of this order prevail in the great sense of ceremony and heraldic display offered in London's colorful rituals and celebrations.

London city is physically large and extended, its districts are very distinctive, and they cluster contiguously around the Thames River, a wide, majestic meander. The locations of railroad stations define their boundaries. King's Cross and Euston Stations to the north, near Bloomsbury; Paddington Station to the west in Bayswater; Liverpool to the east, near the city; Victoria Station to the southwest, adjacent to the Chelsea and Knightsbridge districts; and Buckingham Palace, are all situated on the north bank, and Waterloo and London Bridge Stations are located on the south bank of the river. The meander seems to have shaped the city, whose origins existed before or during the ancient Roman empire. In its continuous evolution throughout medieval times to the present, London's long and colorful history is denoted and defined by its architecture, as permanent a visual documentary as exists. Sovereigns and their reigns are represented in the Tudor-style architecture of Inigo Jones, the Regency period by John Nash, St. Paul's Cathedral designed in 1750 by Christopher Wren, and the Parliament buildings' Perpendicular style.

The medieval character of streets that meander or originate from nodal points is retained in the many squares throughout the city. Trafalgar Square, Belgrave, Grosvenor, Picadilly Circus, Pall Mall are distinctive places. Containing monuments and sculpture, they exist as landmarks of prevailing identity—their place names themselves elicit associations—as well as serving as significant points of orientation.

Large areas have been left to gardens—Regent's Park, Kensington, Hyde Park, St. James Park—the British are renowned for their love of gardening. These urban oases, their grasses thickened and lush from an abundance of moisture, and luminous with green, are the largest areas of color in the city.

In visual memory London's architecture is dark. Facade cleaning in recent years should probably have restored this image to the neutral colors of stone. A city of great bookstores and theater, there is a quality of interiority to its life. Its rich literary traditions have been continuously vital; this is the home of Byron, Keats, Shakespeare, Tennyson, Thackeray, Dickens, Virginia Woolf, E. M. Forster. The English language derives from both Latin and Anglo-Saxon sources. Its vocabulary is enriched by the nuanced differences in meaning among word options, and therefore is larger than that of any other language. The tradition of rhetoric in England prevails in the excellent training of actors and in its unrivaled repertory theater.

Traditions pervade the culture of London, where the role of color is relegated to ceremonial display. The polychrome of shields and standards, the gilt and hued adornment of symbols are medieval in origin, and visible in London's ceremonies and monuments and within its architecture. Here the use of primary reds, blues, and gold are distinctive. Representing placement within an ordering of hues, these colors may have served as an attribute of placement in hierarchy as well. In addition to the associations ascribed to

4-9 Pulpit, London

individual hues, the primary triad may have represented hierarchic position in Britain's heraldic codes.

If the cultural revolt of the 1960s produced the Beatles, the visual signs of pop culture's influence also appeared in the colors applied to London's doorways. The subdued palette brightened to reflect the trendiness of the times. Whether "pop culture" represents a genuine expression of the vernacular, or the promotion of commercial interests imposed upon popular taste, remains a question. On the whole, however, if Paris is recognized as a "grande dame," then London's character remains soberly masculine.

4-10 Cambridge University, England

CAMBRIDGE, ENGLAND

The town exists entirely as the site of its ancient and renown institution, Cambridge University. If London contains wonderful bookstores, then Cambridge's are larger, more specialized, and for its relative size as a city, more numerous. The medieval character of its streets—small, meandering, comprised of buildings small in scale—is a physical model for an interiorized life of the mind.

There are two main streets whose names change. King's Parade becomes Trinity and then St. John's further north. Magdalene turns into Bridge, intersects with St. John's, after which it is Sidney Street, St. Andrew's Street, and on to Regent Street, south toward the train station. The river Cam extends along the town's most open space, the Backs. The university buildings are scattered throughout, physically and historically. Some date to the

thirteenth century, others were the legacy of kings, and some are modern. They represent a series of twenty-five colleges, built around cloisters or courtyards. Trinity College, founded by Henry VIII, is the largest; Sir Isaac Newton, most notably, was one of Trinity's alumni. Its library was designed by Christopher Wren. King's College is known for its chapel, a glorious example of Perpendicular Gothic. Among its alumni were E. M. Forster and the economist John Maynard Keyes. John Harvard, an alumnus of Emmanuel College, was the founder of Harvard University. His predecessors, the Pilgrims who emigrated to America, founded Cambridge, Massachusetts, in the name of their alma mater.

Richness and density are encoded in the physical town, in the architecture, in which traditions are embedded. The medieval character of the university lies in its interiority, in the cloistered privacy of individual thought.

4-11 Central Cambridge, England

Academic rituals reflect long traditions, the expressions of history; they are the occasion for display. Ceremony and informality combine in the society of Cambridge. The visual arts and visual culture per se are not significantly represented; generally, they do not matter much here. But the cultivation of mind and spirit does include music, and music is made by the members of the university themselves, as much the expectation of the academic community here as is doing science or reading literature.

4-12 Street in Old Town, Stockholm

STOCKHOLM

The visual response to a relative diminution of atmospheric light can be complex and unpredictable. At latitude 59 ⅓°, and longitude 18 ½°, the city of Stockholm is located at a global position such that, at midsummer, the Sun never quite sets. Its angle of incidence at this point is so acute that it appears to lie near the horizon, and scarcely hovers below it at nightfall. The consequence to the visual atmospherics is dramatic.

Stockholm is located on the eastern coast of Sweden, open to the Baltic Sea. A city of about one and a half million people, its Old Town is small and dense, comprised of winding streets of connected facades. Its atmosphere moody as a Strindberg play, this

district is the home of Swedish artists and intellectuals. If connections can be made between the physical environment and its psychological effects, this city in shadow seems to have exerted its influence on its artists and thinkers, as well as on the vernacular "eye."

An acute angle of light creates long shadows. When cast upon the surfaces of buildings, the physical wavelengths are visible as hues of the warm, long end of the spectrum. In the Old Town of Stockholm these are reflected from the hard surfaces of window glass and those of more permeable stuccos or stones. Every surface appears bathed in warm amber light. By contrast, the shadows are deep and dark. Windows become wells of blackness and the cobblestones of pavements are harshly articulated. Where streets wind, relative to the Sun's

4-13 Square in Old Town, Stockholm

source, they reflect or absorb its wavelengths. Within enclosed spaces, or a tightly organized grid, shadows may prevail perpetually. The vernacular response to these conditions in the Old Town occurs in its abundant coloration, where colors are applied to buildings that recall the reflected hues of sunlight. Overall, Stockholm, a city of deep shadows contrasting with light, is as warmly colored as Italian towns. Redolent of yellow and green ochers, pink-reds, warm earthy hues, the streets of the Old Town seem to capture the brief presence of warm sunlight, recalling its hues by maintaining them on the surfaces of its buildings.

The visual counterpoint between the sharp separation of light and shade, and warm hues in Stockholm was an unexpected discovery. The mind's image of a Scandinavian city in a northern environment had conjured palettes of cool and neutral color relationships. Instead, the Swedish response to environmental conditions differed diametrically from this preconception. In consequence, the tension effected between the polarization of shadow and light and the harmonic resonance of coloration create a uniquely eloquent environment. The evocative, somber, and reflective mood in the Old Town is highly reminiscent of the cinematic feeling in the great works of its master filmmaker, Ingmar Bergman. He effectively describes the visual qualities of Stockholm through the lens of the camera. More fundamentally though, his themes and characterizations reflect psychological attributes shaped, perhaps, by the eloquent mood of the city itself.

4-14 Store window, Stockholm

4-15 View of Copenhagen

COPENHAGEN

Situated south of Stockholm, at latitude
55 ¼° longitude 12°, open to the Oresund,
and at the eastern boundary of the Sjaelland,
Copenhagen is Denmark's principal city. This
cluster of landmasses includes Jutland, thrust
outward into the North Sea from continental
Europe, about 1° degree north of Germany.

The architectural character of Copenhagen is
Hanseatic, of European influence. The central
city is small and contains pedestrian passageways, like the Stroget, a walkway that connects
shops with historic squares such as the City
Hall Square with King's New Square. Its major
arterials are lined with bicycle lanes throughout the city, permitting the use of two wheels
rather than four, within safe parameters.

Copenhagen is open to the sea. A major
passageway is the inner harbor, which bends
around the Christianborg Palace and has the
character of a street lined with buildings. The
popular landmark, Tivoli Gardens, is 150 years
old and is far more sophisticated in design
than contemporary Disneyland. Situated
within the old city, it is accessible on foot.

On the whole the atmosphere of Copenhagen
is overcast, cool, and restrained in visual mood.
Its old building, the Bourse, constructed of a
somber dark red brick, contrasts with the
painted facades of row houses, predominantly
light in value and cool in hue. If Stockholm as a
city is painterly in effect, then the visual quality
of Copenhagen is graphic.

5-1 Pond at Ryoan-ji, Kyoto

COUNTRY
IN SHADOW:

JAPAN

Japan is comprised of a group of islands between the North Pacific Ocean and Sea of Japan. Geologically young and culturally ancient, its volcanos are active, as are the dynamics of its earth-plate tectonics. It is covered with profuse vegetation, mountains and hills are masses of green, trees and shrubbery cling tenaciously to the earth, and foliage tends to be very small in scale, tightly integrated into larger masses over hills and canyons. The sky is a filtered grayish blue, light rather than bright in intensity. Cloud masses are low to the ground, and they move rapidly. Just after dawn, mists arise from the valleys and drift over the peaks of hills, merging with the clouds. The depiction of these masses of air and hills, in traditional Japanese paintings, quite accurately portrays the effect, monochromatically: areas of mountains as edges overlapped by white space, the "emptiness" of air light. The atmospherics of an island, misty, damp, overhung with clouds, is the physical setting.

5-2 Rooflines in Kyoto

5-3 Detail of rooftiles

The light sense arises then, in conditions of lowered luminosity, and this has affected the earliest traditions of color in architecture. The prototypical tiled roofs of Buddhist temple structures, huge extensive masses, overhang their wooden structural supports and visually as well, areas of landscape. They are open to the sky and curved at the edges. The sequencing of overlapping half-circles form curved striations of glazed ceramic. This shaped plane faces the heavens in a continuum of surface, accepting the light from many possible angles of incidence. The color of the ceramic is a near-silver gray, partly matte, part reflective. In morning light, when the short wavelengths

5-4 Todai-ji Temple, Nara

prevail, they reflect a blue-violet hue from the sky. As the clouds pass, the gray, occluded, darkens—then brightens suddenly, reflecting back the Sun's light. This oscillation between reflection and absorption is very subtle. In the context of deep, richly textured mountain foliage, the roof emerges, flashes momentarily to silver, then sinks into shadowy violet. It is the most complex, yet subtle surface effect of color/form in my experience.

The use of wood in ancient Shinto traditions, appears in the many small shrines and in the Torii, or freestanding apertures found

5-5 Temple base, Sanjusangen-do

5-6 Torii, Kyoto

the consequence of its individual history. Thus, while the structural systems may be similar from temple to temple, each one stands apart as a document in time, affected by the natural conditions of its surroundings.

Of all of the categories defined by the civilizations described here, the one most characteristic of Japanese architecture is the aperture. First of all is the freestanding gate, which in both the Shinto and Buddhist traditions is the primary feature of a temple complex. The gateway marks the principal cardinal point of orientation and the entrance, therefore, to the compound. It can be proportioned beautifully to the human body, the square to rectangular shapes of the simpler Shinto Torii, or the elaborate and monumentally scaled gateway of the Buddhist temple, Chion-in, at Kyoto. These are immense in size, dwarfing the human being, and entirely framing the distant temple to the approach. A version of the temple itself, the gate may have pillars and large, wooden doors, and it supports the huge, heavy tiled roof, the characteristic shape of the temple that is visible from great heights or distances. At Nara the great aperture to Todai-ji is adorned by wooden and polychromed guardian figures, larger than life-size and ferociously and symmetrically framing the aperture itself.

There are no facades. The concept of a wall plane is that of a transparency. The traditional vernacular house is a series of flexible spaces, open to the natural surroundings. Screens separate these spaces. Some, of wood frame, are paper, permitting translucency within the dwelling space. The modulation of light in these interior spaces is a unique aesthetic. As ambient light shifts and changes, the spaces within undergo changes in luminosity and, consequently, appearance. The compositions of light and shadow are echoed in the choice

throughout the cities. Wood is the building material of the large-scale Buddhist temples, and for most of the sculpture that adorns them. The quality of wood, its patina, the consequence of age and weathering, rather than the surface treatment, staining, painting, or varnishing common in the West, imparts a unique distinctiveness to these structures. Conditions of weathering over time differ concretely from place to place; hence no piece of wood has the same appearance, but is instead

5-7 Aperture to Buddhist temple, Kyoto

of materials. The restraint of wood color, reduced to monochrome in juxtaposition with translucent paper, incurs dark delineations against a light, luminous field. This preference for monochromatic composition is evident also in traditional Japanese scroll painting. The coding of natural fluctuations of light and shadow in the surrounding landscape has been integrated here into buildings. In these traditions of architectonic form the interplay of natural rhythms predominates over spatial preconceptions. A flexible architectural system, responsive to concrete conditions of time and place, permits the occurrence of the momentary, giving rise to a supremely perceptual art.

The grill is a feature of the front of a house. Within an enclosing wall, separating the dwelling from the street, the grill permits limited vision from within outward and vice versa, and it is one of the planes of apertures through which one must pass to enter an interior. The scale of houses is small, measured in plan by the module of the tatami, comprised of three, five, or a multiple of these rectangular floor mats. The heights of spaces are similarly small. So are the streets. Hence, in a domestic district, the system of screens and apertures functions to separate the house from the immediate environment, to provide privacy, yet at the same time permit the ceremony of entrance through the aperture. Once within,

5-8 House, Kyoto

5-9 Grill in temple garden, Kyoto

the plane defining the boundary of a dwelling with its garden becomes transparent. Here the entire structure is open to the natural surroundings, and the garden is highly articulated and designed as an entity, to symbolize completion, or the universe. It is an intrinsic part of the architecture.

Aesthetic sensibility in Japan is informed by Nature. The landscape itself is beautiful, compact, and dense with foliage and shrubbery. The genius of the Japanese ceremonial garden, that of the temple, teahouse, or aristocratic dwelling, is its close integration with the natural surroundings. The garden appears artless, yet is constantly maintained. As similar to vegetation in a natural state as is possible, the cultivation of the garden, the pruning and shaping are done with a sense of natural conformation; how a plant wants to grow in a given situation conditions the decision. Unlike the formal landscaping of the French garden, with its laws of symmetry superimposed on "wild nature," or topiary pruning of shrubbery, Japanese shrubs appear to be untouched natural forms. The harmony of the garden within—not only its architectural context as part of the house, but also its relation to the surrounding hills and valleys, the larger

natural environment—is striking. An aesthetic that conforms to nature's subtle designs, rather than superimposing upon them a human system, is evident in these gardens, which, however ancient they may be, appear to the eye in the condition of the moment. I saw how carefully they are tended—debris is swept daily; mosses are brushed; watering is judicious; pruning, though unobtrusive, takes place.

In the traditional teahouse, branches of trees, aged but not treated, are used as a part of the structure of the supporting wooden frames. A reminder of the original source of the construction, these appear as living surfaces with a gnarled or twisted branch extended as a frame to reach another support. Its rhythm changes the uniformity of the other wooden surfaces, planed and sanded, themselves untreated. The quality of the wood, its satiny finish, the consequence of human hands touching and rubbing its surface over time, is appreciated aesthetically, for its shape, texture, and color. The aging of wood, the darkening and exposure of its grain over time is particularly valued. The freestanding apertures or gates found on roadsides have heavy wooden doors that are open to passage; very simple, almost blackened by weathering and time,

5-10 View of Kyoto

these are valued for their altered appearance. Nature's interaction in all senses—the rhythm of time, changes in atmospheric conditions, play of sunlight upon surfaces—is evident in the built forms of Japanese traditional architecture.

The siting of temples is striking in this regard as well. The context of a temple complex is as much a part of the experience of a special, sacred place as the buildings are themselves. The views of temples within landscapes are archetypes of Japanese and Chinese scroll paintings. The temple is nestled within the landscape, appearing against a mountain slope or within a cluster of trees. The spatial

metaphor is that of built form as a part of Nature. I was unprepared for the size of these temples. They are enormous on-site, as are their surroundings. Proportioned to conform to the scale of the particular place, the great gate at Chion-in frames the temple beyond through its central aperture; the distance between these structures is proportioned to this line of sight. The Silver Pavilion, on the other hand, is relatively small in scale, like the delicate mountainous terrain of its setting, with its small-scaled vegetation, and the dry garden, a model of the universe, also relatively small in area. It is as if the natural context itself were selected because it offered certain spatial configurations to the eye, and the architecture was

5-11 Temple garden

then adapted, in scale, and constructed with specific response in size and scale to that site.

At the temple of Ryoan-ji I looked at the pond as I walked around its perimeter, and noted that from every position a composition of the natural context had been made. Framing of photographs became a question of positioning the camera to include a particular portion of the composition. All of it had been carefully observed, then adapted to form a harmonious grouping, or whole. The sense of observation, the detail fitting the context, the alteration of a visual element, after a long process of seeing, is evident in these traditional buildings and gardens. It is a quiet aesthetic, without the egoistic intrusion of individual taste or superimposition of a willful form on the part of a designer. Rather, the meditative contem-

plation of the forms in the landscape itself seems to give rise to the decisions of placement, size, and scale. Finishes, applied surfaces, paints, or stains would, of course, represent interference with the natural processes of change over time; the chance events that might alter, accrue, or subtly color natural materials themselves are preferred.

The aesthetic of the natural is thoroughly embedded in this tradition, and appears in the old streets of town in the vernacular. Houses and shops, made of wood, are similarly left to age, and attain a wonderfully velvet patina that alters in appearance with the angle of sunlight, or in rain.

The sense of color may be influenced by observations of Nature in its subtle changes.

5-15 Wood

5-14 Wood

On the whole the atmosphere and lower luminosity evoke darker, more neutralized color experiences. The foliage appears as deep, dark greens in forests. Against a sunlit field, young stalks of rice can appear transparent, a young yellow-green to mustard color illuminated from behind by a low-lying Sun. The matté tea used in the traditional tea ceremony results from a process of refinement—the youngest tips of tea leaves, free of stems and cleaned of residues, are ground into a very fine powder, producing a green absolutely unique to Japan. It is imitated on the surfaces of the cars of the Japan Railway—a warm, subtly shadowed matte-green (the macerated brew tastes slightly smoked, and rich in its froth on the sides of the tongue), an organic, flowery green—favored in the vernacular.

5-16 Moss, temple garden

5-17 Silver Pavilion, Kyoto

The subtlety of Japanese color lies in its ambiguity. Whereas the Western eye seeks a target hue when experiencing a mixture, for example, *steel* blue, rather than steel *blues,* the Japanese eye seems to accept or tolerate the ambiguity of a color. The stuccoed walls of vernacular houses in newer districts of Kyoto or in outlying towns are painted with neutrals. These grayed colors, high to middle in value on the Munsell scale, are complex neutrals, celery-gray, grayed ocher, or gray yellowish-white, tans of all variables from brownish to green to yellowish tinge—all mixtures neutralized by the influences of several hues. In clusters they appear harmonic in relation to one another. A modern variant of the ceramic tile roof is colored more boldly. Sitting like caps atop these miniature buildings, they are indigo—deep, rich, and nearly black, or a lightly stained bright greenish-blue—or a rich orange-mustard, deep purplish-red, pumpkin-brown, dark chocolate-purple, moss green, and occasionally gray. These roof colors contrast with the stucco walls; for example, gray tile is juxtaposed with light tan stucco, or with smokey-pink walls. The range of wall colors lies within neutrals, contrasting with the rooftops saturated with richer and darker hues when seen from above or clustered in groups. Lively but restrained color is keyed to the generally grayed, light blue of the sky. This vernacular example of color usage is highly sophisticated. Brightly saturated colors do not appear in these towns, and if used in large areas such as signs, they appear raw and ugly, out of context. I noticed that signal yellow, the color used to bisect roads, in Japan is orangey-pumpkin yellow rather than the cadmium yellow medium lines that strip highways in the West. In general, the conditions of lowered luminosity of ambient light significantly influence the color sense. Deeply saturated hues appear relatively bright in the cool luminosity of the environment.

Refined and subtle hues are found also in clothing. Indigo is the color of the robes of Buddhist monks, and the cloth is dyed in a complex series of operations that enhance the depth and intensity of the hue, giving an effect of layering the dye hue within the fabric's threads. Silks, which take dyes beautifully and reflect light in their sheen, are still worn. Western clothing is now commonplace, but the taste of mature women for subtle, deep colors in their woolen suits and jackets is prevalent. The traditional kimono is worn by elderly women, in elegant, rich brocades, small in scale when patterned. Men wear dark blue or brown suits, uniformly, with very conservative neutral or white shirts. Even in the daily workplace, for the salaryman, a preference for refined, subdued color prevails.

The great ceremonial kimonos displayed in museums are more daring in color, with combinations that are dissonant as well as subtle. The Japanese terms for "beauty" have two divergent expressions. *Shibui,* from a root word meaning astringent, signifies a beauty through reduction, a process of simplification and refinement. *Hade,* on the other hand, conveys the sense of the beauty of brilliance—in the kimono, the effect of gold embroidery

against bright vermilion silk. Ideally, these two divergent concepts merge in the aesthetics of color; in concrete examples, there are exquisite silk fabrics that combine delicacy of scale and shape in their decoration with daring and dissonant color relationships.

The influence of Nature again is relevant in these fabrics, most obviously in its appearance as thematic decoration. Flowers, foliage, birds, and insects are the sources of imagery. The affinity for pattern, and the tightness and delicacy of scale, which characterizes much of Japanese "decorative arts," lies, I think, in their perception of Nature. In Japan, species of shrubbery tend to produce small, but numerous foliage. The size and delicacy of natural forms are everywhere in evidence in the natural environment itself. The Japanese are great observers of Nature and its presence in the surroundings may have influenced an aesthetic of delicacy, as well as the tendency to form the patterns found in fabric design and lacquerware decoration.

By contrast with a New England forest, which presents abundant, but massive foliation to the eye, Japanese forests are smaller in scale and in detail, and tend to appear patterned. Shrubs show their shapes in their entirety, branches appear blackened and clearly delineated against the masses of green leaves. Forests of bamboo, a relatively simple form with vertical shoots from which large, pointed leaves emerge, can be seen articulated individually, rather than as masses, even from a fast-moving train. The scale and shapes of mountains, similarly, are relatively small, and within the visual range of the human eye, visible in their entirety. Finally, the intimacy of contact with Nature is made possible by the limited geography of the islands; from no

5-18 City of Kyoto

place is the natural very distant or inaccessible. The affinity for Nature, expressed by traditional architecture in the love of wood, and the complete integration of the garden into the context of buildings was widely in evidence in old Japan.

The sense of refinement in everyday life remains evident also in public manners; the sense of form in human interactions requires bowing in all encounters. In public spaces, on trains, and on buses people dispose of trash in receptacles, and decorum is the order of human transactions in public generally. All the more remarkable, considering the relative crowding of the population, the city of Tokyo contains thirty million people.

Contemporary Japan presents an altogether different face. Tokyo, largely destroyed in World War II, has been almost entirely constructed during the last 50 years. There is a significant disconnection from the traditions of the past, and a wholesale embrace of contemporary commercial culture. Industrial buildings on the outskirts of Tokyo are huge and gleaming white, appearing nearly space-age in form and color. In the central districts of the sprawling metropolis high rises attain the limit of ten storeys; for the most part, restrictions are imposed by the instability of geology—the tendency to experience earthquakes. Glistening newly, their surfaces reflect the Sun; to metal and glass facades are added the glaringly garish colors of global commercial advertising. Buildings in the Ginza, Tokyo's Fifth Avenue, outdo Disney in presenting huge signs, some three-dimensional, others electronic, in constant pulsation of light and color. Clearly here *Shibui* has entirely given way to *Hade*, as the values of a unique culture have been erased to be replaced by the global currency of the present.

5-19 Commercial facade, Kyoto

Unlike Western cities, Tokyo is clean and maintained. During recession, I saw public works projects under construction, streets open to jackhammers, replacing vital infrastructures. In the early morning, elderly women with short-handled brooms appear to sweep clean the surfaces of streets in front of stores in the heart of the city. These contradictory rhythms are juxtaposed. The crowding of the streets on the main arterials tends to be orderly. Cars, trucks, and buses obey the signals; pedestrians pause and wait for walk signs. Their periodicity is well calculated and more efficient than those of American cities. Theirs is, after all, a twenty-first-century city, without the residues of the nineteenth's technology. The efficiency of the transportation systems is admirable. The trains run everywhere, and their nexus at Tokyo Station is more complicated than any in my experience. It is as if all the subway systems in New York, combined with Amtrak, the Long Island Rail Road, as well as the proposed subway to J.F.K. and La Guardia airports, were converged to meet at one place. Incredibly, the trains run and arrive on time, often to the minute. A more coherent signage system, and one displaying number of languages, including English, would greatly enhance the visitor's passage through the complexities of this system.

5-20 Restaurant in Gion district, Kyoto

5-21 Tokyo

5-22 Interior of Kyoto Station

It is evident that the technological present has been fully embraced in Tokyo. Without the living presence of the past, as exists in old cities in the United States and Europe, the Japanese have created, from scratch, an entirely new built civilization. Adapted to the new conditions and materials, a generation of Japanese architects, such as Isozaki and Maki, has infused their buildings with perceptual sensibilities as refined and subtle as their traditions.

CITY STREETS

The appearance of a city is most immediately evident in its streets, in close proximity to its surfaces. Before a conceptual pattern is apprehended or has organized the visual field, the pedestrian perceives the concrete qualities of light and shadows, the colors and textures as they appear on buildings. Their height and styles, as well as their condition and function can be assessed at this scale. The mind's eye takes visual measure of these parameters; their comparison provides the essential distinctions of city quality.

A common supposition is that streets look alike in all cities. To its citizens the *function* of the city is paramount. In usage all streets become linear continua; rows of connected buildings are partially visible at street level, or in their entirety, depending upon the city's density. Their character and flavor are revealed in city districts, developed for different purposes. Whether domestic, commercial, or industrial, the story of a district is told in the style and embellishment of its streets. The history of a city is embedded in its facades, and its active periods may be recalled by their restoration. A district or neighborhood may be well maintained or in a state of decay, clearer symptoms when examined by proximity. More significantly, given the formal constant, a street makes a measure of comparison in color and light possible between the cities that have been represented and are documented here.

Color plays a role in organizing the continuum of facades on a street. Harmonic groupings, adjacent to one another either in hue or value, can create the sense of flow. An abrupt change in contrast will signal the eye, draw attention to the place, and change the rhythmic pattern. If accomplished by design, this continuum may be orchestrated, as are musical phrases, stimulating the ear with harmony or dissonance. The mood of entire districts is affected by limiting the use of color within streets, as is the case in Old City, Stockholm. There zoning ordains the colors that may be used when repainting a facade. Color has a direct sensory appeal to the perceptions; it can shape and enhance, or disturb and irritate. Its usage in streets can be as much a matter of civic behavior as it is the concern of aesthetics.

6-1 Venetian passageway

When colors are used in large areas, on streets or in city districts, they imbue the entire urban field with the sensation of colored light. They also contextualize other colors that may occur within their midst. As a background color will influence the appearance of a small area placed within it, so will the introduction of a contrasting color be influenced by its surroundings. A single facade in contrast with the urban field may function unintentionally as a harsh or dissonant visual event.

The abiding arbiter in making color choices should be the *context*. A designer needs to analyze the city environment, the surrounding buildings, and above all the quality of light in the particular place. Vernacular choices seem to arise after long periods of observation, and are collective. While a designer may not make decisions by committee, it is important that he or she become aware of local constraints upon the individual selection of color and be sensitive to the impact it may have on a building facade or street. Arbitrary choices or self-expression can have unintended consequences on the urban pattern. Designer, beware!

6-2 View of the Campanile

6-3 Light and shadow define a Venetian street

6-4 Venetian "pop" facade

More characteristically than its streets, Venice is defined by a network of canals. Essential to the city's romantic image, these are nonetheless functioning waterways throughout the urban pattern, a delivery system for goods and services. Pedestrian walks run alongside the canals, enlarged to become piazzette in some districts, or connected by bridges to spatially bind the labyrinthian sequence together. No other city offers to the walker the visual variety of adventure and surprises as does Venice. My perambulations over time through its streets have probably amounted to a couple of hundred miles, yet at each turn Venice continues to reveal a new sight.

In the heart of the city, near the Piazza di San Marco a district containing a sequence of very narrow passageways creates parallel perspectives of spatial walls, sliced vertiginously by light or perpetually in shadow.

Once, by accident, through a very narrow gap between buildings, I found a minuscule street, known by the gondolieri to be accessible only by water, and discovered a tiny trattoria perched along its edge. It declared its menu by painted images of prosciutto, salsiccia, pane e vino on its facade, long before the advent of "pop art." On subsequent visits to Venice I was unable to trace my steps to find it again.

The edge, or visual boundary, is a condition of Venetian streets, replete as they are with arches and colonnades. Across streets, listing buildings are buttressed by archways which, as structural elements, provide mutual support.

6-5 Ca'd'Oro, Grand Canal

6-6 Supporting Venetian arches

Along the Grand Canal, the fourteenth-century palazzi were constructed in rows. Ruskin wrote, "Whether noble or merchant... every Venetian appears at this time to have raised his palace or dwelling house upon one time... the forms and mode of decoration... were universally alike; not servilely alike, but fraternally... the likeness of the members of one family. The windows have the noble cusped arch of the fifth order... 'pure Gothic' of the fourteenth century."

Their apertures tie together the "fraternally" designed dwellings in a linear continuum of marble arabesques, drawing the eye from place to place. Repetition and layering are features of their design. Supported by stone pilasters, the organically connected half-round arches repeat as a trefoil or quatrefoil layering, interstices that punctuate the linear motions that enclose them. The variety and complexity of these Gothic traceries were the product of the human imagination and the skill of the stonecutter/sculptor, part repeated formulaically, part invented. The curve, the circle, and the arch, doubled and sprung back upon itself, are rhythmically repeated throughout the city. Stimulant to the eye and foot, the individual is drawn through Venetian streets by the theme and variation of the continuum of tracery. Of white or light marble, the color of the arches and colonnaded balconies contrasts prominently with the facades.

6-7 Palazzo on the Grand Canal

6-8 Gothic facades on the Grand Canal

6-9 Tintoretto red

While only traces remain today, the facades of buildings were once faced with semiprecious stones and contrasting marbles. White marble from Istria, purplish porphyry and green serpentine were wrought in the fifteenth century on the facades of the Grand Canal. The Ca'd'Oro, today a building of grey-white marble, shimmering by reflection in the canal, was once covered entirely with gold leaf, a visual conception staggering to the imagination. In place of precious materials, paint adorns the palazzi on the Grand Canal today. Purple-reds, redolent of porphory, golden ochers, and rich neutrals present their facades to the waterway, weathered to softness. Richness of surfaces, the byplay of light and color, was not limited to the streets of the elite. Throughout Venice the surfaces of the plainest facades are embellished with color. Districts can be identified by the pre-

6-10 Middle-class neighborhood in Venice

dominance of color groupings; in one, an entire street is painted a Lombard red. In a middle-class neighborhood, individual character is maintained between connected houses, two and three storeys in height, by the subtle differences in ochers applied to their facades, green-gray next to neutral adjacent to yellow ocher. Related closely in value, the light facades are unified as a group. Rectangular apertures articulated by white are repeated as shapes throughout the district. Though more modest in material and form than the characteristic marble Gothic arch, they perform the same function, tying together a visual sequence that integrates the neighborhood's streets.

6-11 Baroque church in Piazza Navona, Rome

SPACES AND STREETS OF ROME

This eternal city is a solid city. Unlike Venice, afloat phantasmogorically between sky and sea, Rome is seated among its hills, rooted in earth and ancient stone, in the very physical foundations of its history. The presence of the human figure is ubiquitous—in the marble adornments of fountains, as effigies of pagan gods, or as life-sized saints emerging from the niches of baroque facades. Throughout the city, the human image is tangibly and repeatedly asserted.

Baroque style *is* the interplay of stone and space. Heavy cornices hover over the wave formations of church facades; they crowd into the narrow passageways of ancient streets. This rhythm of figural elements enter the limited spaces in competition with the moving pedestrian, even with the motorcyclist. Weave and bob becomes the urban rhythm of its living inhabitants. The rooflines of great palazzi hang overhead also, defining the boundary or urban edge of connected facades with sculpted detail. Massive doorways, reticulated stone, and huge apertures are the visual features of the streets of the central city.

6-12 Colonnade at St. Peter's

By contrast, the open piazza offers relief, a distinction between the crowding of the street, and the generosity of physical distance, air, light, and space. Roman piazze are shapely, uniquely distinctive, and defined by the imagery of their sculptural fountains. All Italian cities contain piazze, but those of Rome are the most numerous and variegated. They define districts, initiate or form terminal points of major streets, and mark the ceremonial spaces before great palazzi or basilicas. The immense formal structure of St. Peter's Square, with its colonnades flanking the Basilica's facade, was designed to encompass massive crowds. It dwarfs the individual as he or she approaches the church, an effect sustained by the false perspective of the colonnades and the immensity of the entry portals— a small section of which the visitor actually uses. On the other hand, for all its elegance, the Piazza Navona is a domestic space, in continuous use, relaxed and informal. Open space in the Mediterranean climate was a feature of Roman and Etruscan urban design.

Like these predecessors, the color of Rome is earthy and swarthy. Etruscan paintings show visages like those possessed by contemporary

6-13 Three-color sequence in urban space, central Rome

6-14 Scale of ochres on a Roman street

6-15 Lungotevere

Romans. The reds appearing in the murals of ruins are the same as those painted on the exterior surfaces of buildings in the streets of the central city today. Earthy, also, is the Roman dialect, its softened consonants, rounded vowels, and pungent vernacular are supported by gesticulation. Expressive, sensuous, and direct is the urban aesthetic of the Roman vernacular.

Romans orchestrate the color of their streets as continua of surfaces. As is the case in many Italian cities, the color of stone and marble may dominate streets containing church

facades or palazzi. In the Piazza Navona, the buildings surrounding the cathedral tend to mimic the neutral coloration of stone, shaping an entire side of the long, elliptical boundary. Turned on its short axis, however, the colors on building facades here increase in their intensity to the ruddy hues of the central city. Similarly, on the Corso Vittorio Emmanuele, overall the color climate is grayed, the neutral expression of urban cosmopolitanism. This is true, too, of the spoken language; formal Italian may be heard in official places, while the popular Roman dialect will be expressed in its streets.

6-16 Central Rome

6-17 Medici Chapel, Michelangelo, Firenze

6-18 Loggia dei Rucellai

FLORENTINE ENVIRONMENT

A city of merchants as well as princes, poets, philosophers, and artists, Florence displays architecture that encompasses the markets, guilds, hospices, and grand palazzi of its citizens. Its Gothic and Medieval traditions are visible in the Duomo, the Baptistery, the Bargello, and in the old markets. The Renaissance masters created Santo Spirito, the Pazzi Chapel, the Laurentian Library, the Medici Chapel.

The fusion of humane intellect with spiritual traditions in fifteenth-century Firenze represented a peak of human achievement, which resonated in time and space beyond the physical parameters of this small city. Measure, proportion, scale, human values articulated and limited the size of Renaissance buildings; they defined an aesthetic of relationship more abstractly and, therefore, universally significant.

Physical and metaphysical measure of humankind were the standards sought and expressed in buildings, in art, and within the conceptions of human minds. Poets and philosophers shaped the spirit of the times, and architects, sculptors, and painters, in some instances the same individual, tangibly expressed the forms of the reborn culture. Michelangelo, who designed the Medici Chapel, also carved its monumental sculptures. The conception of perspective may have preoccupied Masaccio, before being graphically expressed by Brunelleschi. Vasari, the critic and aesthetician of the following century, was an architect.

Human genius flowered at the time of the convergence of the rational and spiritual. Art preceeding science developed from the same root, and for centuries the energies released during the Florentine Renaissance found expression in architecture, engineering, painting, sculpture, and medicine—the preoccupations of the quintessential Renaissance mind of Leonardo da Vinci. The personification of an infinitely active and engaged intelligence, in all aspects of human endeavor, represents the peak of human capacities. It has never been repeated. The high achievement in the arts of architecture, sculpture, and painting,

begun during the Florentine Renaissance, informed these arts for centuries afterward and influenced all of Europe and beyond.

A city of modest size, fifteenth-century Firenze was the matrix. Whether the accessibility of an environment of limited scale contributed to the encounters—made possible the serendipitous, as well as more formal, exchanges between its artists and intellectuals—and encouraged the ferment, or whether the enlightened and educated predilections of its noble patrons provided the appreciation as well as the commissions for art, the high arts were sustained, celebrated, and generously supported. Above all, the human spirit seemed to be free to express exuberance, self-consciousness was unaccompanied by self-doubt. In a remarkable moment in cultural history, this modest Italian city-state was the locus of genius, the sustainer of an intellectual and artistic power never again repeated.

6-19 Urban space, Florence

COLORS OF SIENA

Narrow, winding streets climb the hill site of Siena's medieval center. Stone and bricks are the surfaces of the continuous bands of buildings, emitting warm coloration from within the shadows. Light brown or pink-reddish brick, high in value and fine in texture, appear in the Campo to unify the space.

Painted facades intermix with these materials on edifices in the surrounding neighborhoods.

These earthy yellows are derived from the pigmentation of the local soils. Artists' pigments, from the same source, are chemically changed by heating processes, producing a range of light to darkened and neutralized yellows, denominated as raw sienna, to a variety of red-browns, or burnt sienna. From soils to facades, these familiar hues introduce a modulated, unitary visual field to the variety of volumetric building clusters in Siena. They absorb and reflect the sunlight. In open spaces they imbue the place with warmth—a feature often

6-20 Medieval street in Siena

6-21 Siennas on Sienese facades

6-22 Urban edge, Siena

6-23 Duomo, Siena

lacking within medieval building interiors in winter. The perceptual interplay of warm yellow facades with cool blue bright sky form the crisp visual contrasts of opposing hues in vernacular spaces, as the crenellated edges of sculpted masses of marbles do in ceremonial spaces. They imbue the environment with life as they mark and distinguish Siena with its unique character.

6-24 Church of San Michele, Lucca

6-25 District in Lucca

LUCCA

Lucca was a visual surprise. The heavy ramparts and stone streets evoked a medieval past, but, throughout, the warmth of its coloration tempered the experience of cold and damp that ancient stones can exude. The solidity of its architecture, stable and disposed in its streets and small piazze, surround the pedestrian.

Color here is luminous; preponderantly reddish or rosey, baked-clay facades elicit warmth by association or extend spatially by physical wavelength. The streets form an embrace rather than alienating one. Buildings as clusters are painted similarly, defining small neighborhoods—here a clay-colored group, there a district unified by ochre/umber. To perceptual clarity is added elation, a rare urban *physical* experience.

6-26 Streets in Lucca

6·27 Luminous surface, Bologna

6-28 District in Bologna

COLORS AND
LIGHT OF BOLOGNA

Separated from central Tuscany and Umbria by the Appennine Mountains, the light of Bologna differs from those regions. The city environment is enhanced by its clarity, which in autumn intensifies the glow of color. The reds of Bologna pervade the central city. Fully saturated, earthy iron oxides and ochers influence some mixtures, and facades surrounding city squares resonate with color.

6-29 Bolognese facades

Solid red walls in the luminous field reflect the coloration of those placed adjacent to them. In districts of architectural density the proximity of buildings to one another place facades at angles close in their proximity, causing reflections that radically alter the appearance of a facade. In one, a wall changed from its base to roofline, from ocher to red, effected by light. Juxtapositions of these wall planes, painted close in value but different in hue, produced optical junctures

where distant planes appeared to merge spatially. These magical transformations occur within an urban field of color adjacencies— reds, red ochers, burnt siennas, roseate pinks—close enough in value to add their light to the surface pigmentation of the building. This paradox of solidity in the structure and weight of the architecture with the evanescent transformation of color is absolutely unique to Bologna.

6·30 Mameluke intarsia in Jerusalem

ISRAEL: STREETS AND SPACES

The streets of the Old Town in Jerusalem are synonymous with its spaces. Narrow passageways that follow the configurations of a labyrinth, they climb as they wind. Stairs, consequently, are a feature, and openings into stores or places occur frequently. Arcades capture and modulate light, an attribute of cities in hot, bright climates. Stone surfaces throughout are relieved by the aperture of a window or door, where the color shifts from the texture and neutrality of the material to its essential transformation by light. Embedded in a city wall, a fragment of the Mameluke occupation is visible, a unique intarsia of stones, varied in coloration from warm honey to cool neutral and of curvilinear design. A district where doorways are painted blue is likely to be Arab. The color of heaven, a mystical reference, blue tiles embellish the exterior walls of the Dome of the Rock, and blue is repeated in the symbols surrounding doorways in the Arab sector.

The edge is a feature of Jerusalem's streets. To begin with, the gated enclosure of the walls of the Old City are embellished with ramparts; the crenellated patterns of warm stone towers and walls contrast with the blue sky. Rooftop configurations of domes vary: Moslem hemispheres and Greek Orthodox onion domes, as well as Christian cupolas dot the urban field. Towers and turrets, distributed among the flat surfaces of roofs, engender variety when seen from a bird's-eye view, as well as from street level.

In Bethlehem blue and occasionally green doors occur. Surrounding the immediate area of an aperture, the blue is extended beyond, unevenly painted on the plane of the facade, as if the only significance were the opening itself. A swath of pink partially adorns another building on a Bethlehem street.

Safed, the home of Jewish mysticism, is constructed of stone. Its cool, sere atmosphere is reflected in the streets, and the colors appearing on their facades tend to be yellow. Here also color is applied in a broad swath over the building's facade.

6-31 Rampart Gate to Old Town, Jerusalem

6-32 Street in Bethlehem

MEXICAN FORM AND COLOR

The overlay of the Spanish colonial on the indigenous civilizations influenced the shapes of Mexican towns and streets. The zócalo, or town square, was the plan of aboriginal people, the place of the market and governance. Spanish plazas integrated with the indigenous forms, and in most towns there is one main zócalo, containing the church, a principal hotel and restaurant, and a kiosk, used for meetings and as the site of the local marimba band.

In Mexico, D.F., and Oaxaca the streets extend horizontally; low-lying, one-storey buildings predominate in domestic neighborhoods. Vistas are broad and far-ranging, the landscape is part of the town image. In pre-smog-laden days Popocatépetl once loomed on Mexico City's horizon. In coastal places, such as Tehuantepéc on the Atlantic, at the juncture of shoreline and rain forest, the natural environment heavily influences the shape of the town.

The streets of these cities appear as extended horizontal bands of color against a background of vast sky. In the dry season, at high elevation, its color is a deep cobalt blue. The continuum of pure, saturated colors of small, connected buildings, is balanced by the unbroken expanse of sky, which, unexpectedly, can function as a neutral field. The effect of an extensive sky, contrasting with an active horizontal band below, exposes the eye to maximal color stimuli. Mexicans regularly paint their houses and storefronts, replenishing faded with strongly saturated hues, often without regard for the adjacent building's color. Lime green against magenta, an active contrast, is a stimulant like firecrackers at a fiesta, brass in a mariachi band, or chiles in mole sauce.

Given the relative simplicity of the adobe structure as form, color becomes a shaping factor in the urban field. At the terminus of a street in Oaxaca, a storefront, painted a fully saturated red and blue, punctuates the end of the path just as a period terminates a sentence. In Jalapa, Vera Cruz, bright yellow and blue buildings are placed at the intersection of a street. The eye is carried over the 90° juncture by the repetition of colors to continue in the direction of its path. Repeatedly one experiences the use of color in Mexican cities as a

6-33 Street in Oaxaca

6-34 Street in Jalapa, Vera Cruz

mode of organization or orientation; it vividly shapes environmental spaces and functions as a factor coequal in importance to that of any other element of design.

Colonial towns of Querétaro and Puebla feel more European, with the plaza/church configuration familiar and smaller in scale. White church facades and/or their towers rise over the city's streets, enhanced in brightness by contrast with the sky, and read as landmarks or nodal points. But beyond the plaza, the streets of these towns are as colorful as any in Mexico.

Throughout Mexico, the vernacular is comprised of a combination of solid, simple volumes of buildings, with strong, declarative colors. Form and color are inseparable components of the rows of one-storey structures, constructed low to the ground and connected as street facades. Saturated hues also appear as a formal element, defining a roofline or doorstep, balcony or aperture, often as a substitute for the physical structure itself. In a culture of poverty, strategies of design are devised within the constraints of economy and simplicity. Painted color provides an available, inexpensive solution.

6-35 Intersection of Jalapeño street

With respect to the Mexican love of saturated color, the natural environment, itself a source of polychromed imagery, may have had an influence in a more fundamental way. The high plateaus and mountainous regions in which cities and towns are located are intensely brilliant. In this context, it is evident that the visual system, the eye and brain, responds in kind. It is as if the total level of luminosity in the visual environment requires an accommodation in the visual system itself, a change in its set point or the limits of its parameters.

It has been observed that when color preferences are transplanted from Mexico to Manhattan, for example, they lose the sensory appeal they had originally, appearing in the new environment as harsh and crude. Contrasts that are irritating under median circumstances of light intensity, however, may be tolerable or even preferable within elevated levels of light. The eye and brain respond to local contrasts within a given field. But it may be that given the circumstance of *increased light intensity in the total visual field,* the visual system *appears to change its ratio, or set point, so* that fully saturated colors appear "normal," within the increased range in the parameters of light. An adaption not only to local contrasts but also to the totality of the influence of environmental light may occur.

Luis Barragan, the great Mexican architect, used color as a dimension, and treated it as a formal component in his buildings at the onset and throughout the design process. In a Barragan building redness becomes wall; color is architectonic, not an addition. The fusion between form and color, the hallmark of the architect's work, may be attributed to the influence of a traditional Mexican vernacular. Here the development of an individual formal aesthetic may have had its origins in the expression of popular culture—architecture as art.

With the circumstance of a changed ratio in the visual system it is plausible that an intensely blue sky could behave as a dark field, relative to adjacent, saturated hues, as one witnesses in Mexico. If this were to be the case, then the light of environments, playing a role in shaping the collective sense of color that distinguishes vernacular cultures, might be physiologically based.

6-36 Old Santa Fe Trail, New Mexico

SANTA FE, NEW MEXICO

The town of Santa Fe follows a colonial version of the urban pattern of old Mexico, with a plaza located at its center. The Palace of the Governors is a building dating to the beginning of the original settlement, and it remained continuously in use by its Spanish, Mexican, and American governors until the present, when it was converted to a museum. On market days it is the site of Native

6-37 Arcaded street near Palace of Governors, Santa Fe

American Navajo artisans selling their crafts and jewelry of silver and turquoise. Shops and hotels line its perimeter, the terminus of the Old Santa Fe Trail.

As a center, the streets of Santa Fe self-consciously adapt the style and character of the amalgam of Spanish and Mexican cultures. The color of earth, shapes of adobe, relatively limited size and scale of buildings, the use of patios, and the simplicity of embellishment maintain a consistent visual character. The spare use of color on wooden frames surrounding windows, porches, and trim is limited to blues, turquoise, or sky blues, generally lighter adjacent to their adobe walls as the sky is to the Earth.

Native Americans built adobe structures, housing complexes featuring stacked/stepped units several storeys in height, kivas, and community ovens or kilns of the local clay. Soft and dense sculptural volumes, they sit within the environment, related in substance and color to the earth beneath. Generally they are left unpainted, the color of baked adobe. On churches whitewash may cover a facade to distinguish it from its adjoining towers. Wooden frames of windows and doorways are painted, often light blue, a soft articulating detail. The simplicity of these buildings, their bulk and stability, lend a sense of dignity, quiet, and permanence to the place.

6-38 Painted details, pueblo church

LOS ANGELES: DISTRICTS AND STREETS

Streets in the districts that represent Greater Los Angeles differ over the vast arena of its geography. From the elevation of a freeway, the view of city grids emerge from the blur, often arrested by the ubiquitous four-corner intersection containing a gas station, a car wash, and a minimall or two. With no particular visual character, other than their functions, these L.A. landmarks repeat endlessly throughout flatland, the vast area of basin that constitutes much of the south and central parts of the city.

The urban network of high-rise buildings defines the revived downtown civic and business center in the Hill Street area—a city in the making. Complexes such as the Civic Center, the Contemporary Museum of Art, the Music and Theater Center, appear to float as urban entities in the vast horizontal field of space as one experiences them from the freeway. Wilshire Boulevard, from its origin in Santa Monica, bordering the Pacific Ocean, extends throughout West Los Angeles, Westwood Village, Beverly Hills, West Hollywood, Museum Mile, Wilshire District, eastward downtown, a voyage of more than 2 hours' duration by car. Visually an endless linear continuum of buildings of varying heights and relatively low density, one's chances of parking in front of a destination on Wilshire Boulevard are surprisingly good, a singular bonus in this city of the automobile. In fact, the private vehicle is the only viable option to move from place to place. For the working poor domestic, a bus ride from East L.A. requires rising at 5:00 a.m. in order to arrive in Beverly Hills by 9:00 a.m.

Older districts, such as Santa Monica on the Pacific Coast, are more defined. The terminal point of the great avenues, Wilshire and Santa Monica Boulevards, and of Route 66, one of the continent's oldest highways, connecting Chicago to Los Angeles, Santa Monica's streets were designed initially for the automobile. Ample and broad, they contain sidewalks, absent in many districts elsewhere. The one-storey bungalow, or Spanish-style house, built in the 1920s is a genuine example of Southern California vernacular. The city of Santa Monica is a district of mixed use, comprising an active commercial district, restaurants and theaters, and domestic suburbs.

Brentwood is predominantly suburban, its streets wind and are accessible only by car; its edge, Sunset Boulevard, is settled by large, expensive dwellings, sequestered by landscaping against intrusion. Shopping is done on San Vicente Boulevard, itself a winding path entirely separated from the domestic environment, an excursion by car. North of Sunset lie the mountains and canyons, more rugged terrain on which to build, with dwellings connected by ribbons of mountain passes accessible by vehicle only.

West Hollywood, which Sunset Boulevard traverses, contains its characteristic Strip, the commercial district comprised of upscale shops, restaurants, theaters, and hotels, adjacent to rental car agencies, and minimalls. Signage dominates the area; billboards, some exceeding in height the neighborhood's buildings, assault the eye with a sequence of pop images. Here the Marlboro Man, a billboard giant, becomes a landmark. Advertisements of the latest Hollywood blockbuster take precedence in size and significance over architecture in defining the Strip. Neighboring streets form one of the older districts of Los Angeles. They are comprised of detached, multiple-dwelling, two-storey buildings, mostly unrelated to one another in period or style.

Commentary on the quality of flatness of buildings has been made elsewhere. In the harsh sunlight of an essentially desert region, building facades appear to be paper thin and uniformly illuminated. A variety of borrowed styles embellish these ordinary buildings. Absent a sense of substance, the architecture shows its derived styles by means of graphic signage.

To the east, beyond the City Center with its high rises, a vast, relatively uninhabited industrial zone exists. The site of railroad tracks and one-storey industrial buildings, this almost surreal landscape reflects the urban flatness and extended sense of space of the city. It presents as a site of a continuously expanding horizon, once seemingly infinite in possibilities, the place of beginning again— the western edge of the American dream.

6·39 Bridge over Seine, Paris

6·40 Color continuum of a Parisian street

PARISIAN STREETS AND SPACES

An open city, the streets of Paris appear to carry one to a destination. From its broad boulevards, a serene pace of connected facades of the grand houses draws the eye through their sequence to a terminal point. From there a great monument, a place, or the view of an urban intersection is revealed like a vanishing point, framed by the street.

Bridges begin and end in open spaces; they breathe and they vary. City views are discernible from many positions along the Seine. Its quays have been the vantage point of choice for painters; the French Impressionists particularly created images of its panoramas. Where two boulevards intersect, the architecture at their convergence is rounded or curved, a massive formal terminus.

Against the visual weight of the architecture the color of Parisian streets is light, elegant, and sophisticated. A linear sequence of facades show apricot, beige, rose-neutral, and gray buildings, light to middle within the Munsell scale of values. On another street, a row of green-gray facades show subtle variations in hue. A continuity of surfaces is achieved on the street, despite the distinction of individual facades. Embellishments, cornices, and sculpted details further distinguish buildings from one another, but their heights are absolutely regulated. Generous spatial distances maintained between streets admit the sun. It softly moulds sculptural details, rounds the shapes of cornices, and creates nostalgia.

On the Left Bank, in the district of galleries, antique shops, and bookstores, the color of facades is used as graphic signage. Understated, their blacks, deep browns, indigos, navy blues, and a variety of cool grays face the street, speaking a language of sobriety and high culture. On a corner of the Rue de la Seine a gallery is housed in blond stone. Despite the largely commercial function of this district, its visual character projects the image of sophistication and discretion; with facades of closely related, dark colors its unity is maintained.

6-42 Harmonic color, Parisian street

6-41 Facade, Left Bank

6-43 Alpine street, Parisian color

TOWN IN THE FRENCH ALPS

A street in a small town in the French Alps shows distinctly Parisian colors on its buildings, albeit much smaller in scale.

Apricot, mouse gray, pale yellow neutrals can be compared in their frequency and amount on the town's streets, with those of the capital.

6-44 Blond Burgundian facades

BURGUNDY

The small French town provided a visual surprise. Warm and blond, the streets' facades reflected light yellows and saturated ocher surfaces, with soft green ochers, and delicate bluish grays on their apertures. Tiles on turrets and rooftops of a municipal building comprise an active tapestry pattern of light yellow, red, and black elements. Half-timber construction on the buildings' facades and wooden pillars, small in scale, form a colonnade below. This ancient town is intimate, and speaks with the transitional colors of the Meditteranean.

6-45 Half-timbered Burgundian facade

6-46 Astor Place, New York

THE STREETS OF MANHATTAN

Downtown, midtown, and uptown, Manhattan's visual character was imprinted in the nineteenth century, reached its apogee in the first half of the twentieth, and is negatively affected now by its continuous growth. In the neighborhoods of lower Manhattan the tenement buildings still exist, amidst the lofts of the small factories that once defined the district. Red brick apartment buildings are juxtaposed with facades reinforced with iron. The East Village contains four- and five-storey connected houses with high stoops, mixed with small shop fronts on their first floors. Creative energy is evident in these places, where small entrepreneurs start businesses, fashion designers set up shops, and restaurants of every ethnic variety take root. Individualism is the hallmark of this part of Manhattan, along with its ethnic neighborhoods. As buildings and streets provide a matrix, remaining relatively unchanged, a moving population declares its presence graphically in store fronts and signage.

SoHo is characterized by Broadway, and the streets between this avenue and West Broadway, which contain galleries and lofts, are the southern outpost of the art scene. The integrity of the neighborhood streets is maintained by the limited heights of its buildings, and its facades, which speak of the industrial era. Dynamic, as is the city's economy, the district increasingly attracts corporate chains, trading on the neighborhood's image, and they tend to displace individual businesses. In the crowded and active old textile district there are signs of rehabilitation in the repainting of the old iron-coursed facades—once dark, they are now white. A sense of intimacy with this part of Manhattan is made possible by its relatively moderate scale and high-population density. Adjacent to SoHo is Little Italy, and Chinatown is near TriBeCa, neighborhoods of mixed use, where people live and work as they always have in old cities.

Midtown skyscrapers, the earliest being the Chrysler and Empire State Buildings, dominated the Manhattan skyline in the 1940s. As landmarks today, they depend upon light shows to be made visible among the forest of highrises surrounding them. On the avenues here human scale rapidly diminishes; some cross streets even retain the four- or five-storey buildings original to the district, but individuality has been replaced by the scale and anonymity of the monuments to global commerce. Rockefeller Center, at midcentury a monumental urban complex, appears in their midst today as one of large, but human, scale. Its popular sites, Radio City Music Hall and the skating rink, are actively in use.

Uptown, along the boundary of Fifth Avenue and opposite the Metropolitan Museum of Art, rows of mansions, five storeys in height, overlook Central Park. Restored to cleanliness, their stone facades are uniformly beige in color and delineated by mechanically repeated sculptural detail on window lintels, broad doorways, and heavy cornices at roofline. Architecturally sterile, these facades effect aloof anonymity. A mix of diplomatic and domestic functions, this section of Fifth Avenue, with its proximity to Central Park, might be expected to encourage pedestrian activity. People walk their dogs or jog for exercise here, but all human activity appears to be *purposeful*—none of the aimless wandering or savoring of the place that would occur in similar neighborhoods in great European cities such as Paris or Rome.

Comparisons may be made between upper Fifth Avenue and Commonwealth Avenue in Boston. The broad avenue of Boston's Back Bay is also comprised of rows of attached mansions or town houses, five or six storeys high, but they are constructed mainly of warm red brick or matching stone. Their facades have more individual character in their detailing and are frequently adorned by enclosed front gardens. Once a domestic neighborhood, many Back Bay mansions have been converted to institutional functions such as clubs and private schools. All of the visual attributes contributing to a sense of human scale have been retained after conversion, and consequently the district is active with street life, the lifeblood of urban places.

The streets of Harlem, further uptown in Manhattan, at the beginning of the twentieth century and through the "Harlem Renaissance" comprised one of the most architecturally distinguished sections of the city. Buildings on "Striver's Row," on West 138th and 139th Streets, for example, were designed by Sanford White. Now one of New York City's most blighted neighborhoods, rehabilitation and restoration could recover what had been one of Manhattan's most vibrant districts.

There is little color in Manhattan's crowded urban field. The pervasive neutrality of its buildings is generally warm in tone, but without variation or nuance in hues the facades of its great avenues appear uniform and monotonous. Stone and concrete predominate as materials, glass appears in use on Park Avenue and elsewhere, and brick apartment buildings exist throughout the city. But on the whole, the relative absence of color in Manhattan exacerbates a prevalent sense of anonymity and monotony, especially as its urban fabric becomes more dense.

6-47 Lower Broadway

6-48 Industrial Boston

BOSTON: NEIGHBORHOODS AND CITIZENS

Described frequently as "the hub," the earliest streets of Boston were cow paths, formed at the heart of its seventeenth- and eighteenth-century town plans. They retain a winding pattern. The streets of the downtown business district, comprising the high rises built in the 1960s, commingled with landmark historic buildings such as the Old Statehouse, can be confusing when added to the mix is a relative absence of street signs.

The configuration of Beacon Hill is coherent because of the stylistic consistency of the pattern of town houses that line the streets, four or five storeys high, mostly 18 feet wide, and built of red brick, with white or black detailing. Narrow streets, designed for pedestrian passage, not vehicles, are bounded by narrower brick sidewalks, and black street lanterns, converted from gas to electricity in the last century, remain in use. The steep hill affords views of the Charles River, and the eighteenth-century scale of the colony pervades the entire district. The Statehouse with its gilded dome dominates the hill and rises loftily from Beacon Street, the edge of the Public Common, and downtown Boston, but it does not overwhelm the domestic neighborhood, nor does it alter its sense of small scale. Beacon Hill combines a rare combination of formal urbanism with intimacy.

The urban character of Copley Square, combining a grand version of the New England town square with the European plaza, was more coherent before it became an exit of the Massachusetts Turnpike in the late 1960s, and before the blue-green glass wedge of I. M. Pei's Hancock Tower was built adjacent to the Richardson church. The Boston Public Library's original building was designed by McKim. Opposite the church, it forms the western edge of the plaza, and its addition on Boylston Street, designed by Philip Johnston, is respectful of the integrity of the old building, retaining its scale and color. A public place, Copley Square is in civic use, the site of "First Night" and other popular celebrations. Its open space at the center of Back Bay defines one of the city's most distinctive and beautiful districts, kept so by active citizen participation.

Boston's visual character was shaped by its Yankee past, and their efforts to build and maintain a rich and coherent city is in evidence today. The influence of individuals in the nineteenth century helped create the distinctive institutions and traditions that defined the character of their cities. These legacies are shaping forces to the present time. Often a reflection of high social ideals and civic commitments, as well as a desire to create memorials to their names, individual patronage supported the urban plans of Frederick Law Olmsted, the architecture of Richardson, and the founding of Boston's many cultural, educational, and medical institutions.

The belief that an enlightened environment creates civilizing forces was unquestioned at that time. But it has eroded during this century, along with doubts about the general value of aesthetics and its influence, if any, on urban life. With an increasing indifference in people to the significance of participation in civic life, has come an emphasis on the individual. Paradoxically, the shift of focus from the public arena to the concerns of private citizens has impoverished cities, and deprives an individual of the sense of autonomy, that is, the ability to influence or shape events. Today, "all politics is local," Boston's late, beloved Thomas P. (Tip) O'Neill, Democratic Speaker of the House of Representatives, rightly observed. So are civilizations. They are sustained by functioning cities in all their interactive complexity and tangible, concrete *physical* presences. The sense of belonging begins with a sense of attachment, and this can be discouraged or sustained by the environment itself.

CAMBRIDGE, ENGLAND

The mood, character, and appearance of Cambridge as an academic town is due to its medieval past, qualities marked by the emblematic signs that adorn the facades of gateways to the cloisters of university buildings, as well as by its meandering streets. All elements concur to focus inward, the physical layout sustains inner concentration, perhaps the reading of a book as one peram- bulates. The town's shape evolved around its single function, *learning,* as other medieval towns were by their cathedrals.

The edge is articulated, between the crenella- tions of walls and structures against the cloudy sky, and is visible throughout the city's vistas, where the buildings are limited in height. Tawny surfaces of weathered stone soften any

monumental effect. The grandness of stone has been moderated by lichen and moss, and tempered by time. The entire town has been patinated. Moss green, added to dark moldy brick, are its colors. The somber palette of deep browns, dark green ochers and iron- blacks, becomes the local preference. In town, iron gates and well-polished brass are the details arresting the eye at the bookstore or barbershop.

This is an entirely unselfconscious vernacular. It arises from a feeling of leaving things as they are—weathered, battered, and familiar—and perhaps also from a sense that the appearance of things isn't all that important after all. The consequence of this indifference, paradoxically, is that of a coherent and consistent visual image, with meaning revealed in its appearance and a tendency to linger in memory.

6-50 Stockholm facades

6-51 Street in Old Town, Stockholm

STOCKHOLM: OLD TOWN

The twisting and winding streets of Old Town, Stockholm, playfully reflect or evade the scarce sunlight they receive. The midsummer night's dream of continuous luminosity may be the aspiration of the colors chosen to adorn its walls. To capture that golden warmth, with the imprint of its momentary presence, may be the rationale behind sourcing the hues of southern climates, selected and retained by zoning, to embellish the streets of the town.

Light and dark predominate over color, the consequence of the Sun, positioned low on the horizon, and shadows extended far horizontally. Facades in shadow, luminous with hue, reflect from the dark glass windows opposite them. In a town square shadows conceal, then reveal, its murky parameters. In a shopping district the signage is small, in scale with street size, and those on shops, such as this one selling gloves, are positioned perpendicularly to the surface of the facade, to catch the eye of the passerby. Restrained and simple, the graphics are well integrated with the architecture.

The function of color on the street of connected buildings is to mark the property lines or boundaries separating them. In Stockholm these transitions are subtle; the streets retain continuity and harmony with the use of closely related hues and integrated values, as if the socialist ideals of the culture were reflected in its urban aesthetics.

6-52 Street in Copenhagen

6-53 Copenhagen, street along the canal

COPENHAGEN: SQUARES AND STREETS

The presence of water is felt in Copenhagen. Streets face the canals, which interplay with and shape the urban edge and add a quality of openess to the environment. Sky and sea add their color also to the urban fabric. The sky, a cloudy violet gray, is reflected in the water, closer to indigo. The dark red brick used to build the Bourse is broken by the intervals of vertical dormers and copper piping. A tower is also copper clad, turning verdigris from oxidation, and is topped by a spiral pinnacle resembling a spindle shell. The four-part color grouping, gray violet, vertigris, dark red brick, and indigo, is distinctive of this section of Copenhagen.

Along a canal a street of connected facades reveals a cluster of hues broader in range and more contrasted in value than those of Stockholm. Pale yellow, slate blue, deep orange-ocher, gray, pale blue, and white—these colors separate the buildings sharply and define them individually.

In a commercial district the characteristic perpendicular signage is elegant, spare, and

6-54 Bourse, Copenhagen

small in scale with its surroundings, showing a Scandinavian sensitivity to place. More linear and graphic in quality than the signage found in Stockholm, the Danish sensibility seems to prefer visual contrasts. Even in the popular amusement park, Tivoli, a sense of order and restraint keeps the visual environment elegant and lively, but refined.

FACADES

Facades are the faces of cities; like human faces they vary in character and expressiveness. At close range a building's age, style, or function, inscribed on its surface by its size, material, color, or other visual attributes, becomes noticeable. Collectively, streets are series of facades, and their discordance or compatibility with one another may distinguish a district or neighborhood. For the individual, the immediate connection with place occurs at this scale. Light plays on surfaces, the texture of materials are noticed, signage or other graphic elements engage the eye, apertures in the wall plane become visually significant.

The aperture, doorways, entrances, and windows, is universally distinguished on the facade by a marked shift in color or material. Stone lintels articulate these openings in a wall plane, or paint may differentiate them from their surfaces, depending upon the economics of the vernacular. The contrast in color of a material, its sculpted detailing, or the simple painted highlight confers similar visual significance to places of entry or openings in the wall.

If the facade is a face, then windows and doorways may constitute its features. Noticeably colored on the human face, the eyes and mouth have particular roles to play in the range of expressions and nonverbal communication of their possessor. Although the function of buildings explains the special designation ascribed to its apertures, clearly, an entrance or exit should be markedly differentiated from the wall plane by its size, shape, and color; a ceremonial aspect may be conferred by the special attention as well. A grand entry, or a hidden one, speaks volumes. An open or shuttered window welcomes or retreats. Gratings, gateways, and ironwork covering doors and windows are rarely only decorative. The exclusion assigned by gated communities is a feature of recent upscale housing developments. The significance of the aperture is thus a function of the urban code; one spoken visually and universally.

7-1 French Alps, graphic facade

7-2 Chocolate factory, Mexico

THE GRAPHIC FACADE

The vernacular facade has an expressive function in the graphic storefront. Small entrepreneurs everywhere embellish the fronts of their places of business with signage, or regard the facade itself as graphic.

The sematographic facade is the visual equivalent of the linguistic rebus. Like that aspect of written language, it describes its meaning directly by use of mimetic forms and imagery. In the most sophisticated cities as well as remote towns, the graphic facade speaks the local vernacular with its visual analogue in form and color.

In the French Alps the Picon sign painted on a house clearly declares itself as it dominates the structure; its bold typeface neatly fits the surface and volume of the building. A chocolate factory in a Mexican town says so with a facade featuring a heavy overhang painted chocolate brown. And in Paris a horse butcher advertises with an effigy of the animal's head—a sematographic.

7-3 Venetian palazzo

VENICE

A world power, the Republic's wealth made Venice a cosmopolitan city and sustained it through the late Renaissance. At its height during this period, the great Venetian painters, the Tiepolos, Tintoretto, Titian, and Veronese lavishly embellished the interiors of palaces and churches with images of its doges, allegories, and historic narrative. Its distinctive architecture remains extant, not solely in its churches and monuments, but also in its great palazzi, the Grimani, Rezzonico, Spinelli. The domestic city is extant; its identity is inscribed in Venetian facades in the most immediate, yet permanent documentary medium known—architecture and urban form.

Strolling through the streets and scanning facades, preferably by slow boat, the astute observer takes note of history. Symbols and narrative abiding in tangible form were designed to be read. The "decorative" aspects of sculptural detailing, or the embellishments of architectural facades, attract the attention; the more colorfully, the more effective their drawing power. When art and history combine, visual imagery conveys meaning more immediately than the written word. Having virtually eliminated, or debased, this primary modality in the modern city, we have

7-4 Venetian palazzo

learned to deny its significance. The rich sensorium of the visual arts in Venice presents a shock of the old; the existence of the integration of purpose, spirit, and appearance that both expresses and sustains great civilizations is here in tangible form.

The cathedral of Saint Mark's, representing the amalgam of building over time, is richly embellished with mosaics and a profusion of colonnades on its facade. Ruskin, observing that the columns on the facade of Saint Mark's cathedral were of white alabaster, veined with gray amber with shafts elsewhere against its surface of porphory, alabaster, or fine marble, noted that these were not neces-

sarily structural, but "placed to show their colors in their highest possible brilliancy... without sunshine the wall veil is subdued and varied by subtle gradations of half-shadow"— sculpture for color's sake.

The Ducal Palace was faced with brick-red and cream colored tiles, forming a continuum of fourfold symmetries, which plays against the linear rhythms of the column courses below. Built for the first doge in 820, it was destroyed by fire and reconstructed and enlarged in the twelfth century and, like the cathedral, continued to be modified by later additions.

7-5 Veronese's house, Venice

7-6 Painted facade, Venice

The appearance in the vernacular of the Venetian Gothic arch on the facades of palazzi on the Grand Canal unified the public with the domestic city and recurred through-out its streets. According to Ruskin, these arches were made of iron, and shaped sheets of marble were then overlaid on the intermediate spaces between windows. These veneers are still visible on their surfaces; traces of porphyry and serpentine remain in the fascias and details on some buildings. Other facades were stripped to their foundation brick walls and were plastered and painted. They are colored with the ochers, bisters, roseate/purplish and warm neutral hues of the vernacular, all keyed high to middle on the Munsell scale of values. Subtle yet vibrant, even the neutrals are alive in the reflected luminosity of the lagoon. Related to the hues of the semiprecious stones they replaced, they are particularly eloquent in weathered old age.

Facades in Venice have accrued their coloration over time; like paintings they are layered with impasto. When fresh house paint cannot match the old, tempered appearance, it is left in place. The embellishment of buildings this venerable is in part a function of human memory, and respect is paid when color is renewed. The variety of hues remains within a rich range of colors, reminiscent of those used by the painters of the High Rennaissance, Tiepolo, Titian, and Veronese, whose environ-ment and source Venice was. The gestalt, or collective sense of color, is self-contained and complete, unique to Venice and distinct from other Italian cities. It prevails through centuries much as the local dialect does,

enhancing the sense of place with sensory directness and a specific vocabulary.

The crenellation of forms at the boundary between facade and sky is a distinctive attribute of Venetian playfulness. Domes, towers, cupolas, belfries, obelisks, and cornices abound, a proliferation of forms to stimulate and delight the eye. Their colors, material or applied, cast against a saturated blue sky, form a clear contrast of building edge against natural field. They add to the vocabulary of urban edges represented by the outlines of piazzette shaped against the canals and the sea.

An attribute of color on the vernacular facade is its placement, frontally relative to the street or passageway, with a shift or variant of color applied to the side. Front to side, color used as orientation is part of the Venetian formal color vocabulary, and it appears on the palaces along the Grand Canal, as it does throughout the city. Perhaps a consequence of economics, the fascia of semiprecious materials would be limited to display only on the principal facade, visible from a ceremonial distance or from a gondola. The painted replacements of marbles and stone retain this distinction; common brick suffices for the side. This formal statement is found elsewhere—in Stockholm, in the salt boxes of New England towns, even in Manhattan. Orientation expressed by color or material is a common attribute of the vernacular facade.

The sematographic facade is also a part of the Venetian vernacular. The Clock Tower in Piazza San Marco—headed by the resplendent winged Lion, icon of the city, a gentle Madonna and Child, and the astrologic disk designating the time—is a prominent sign at the city's heart. The entrance to the Academia di Belle Arti is a simple tall and narrow Gothic arch, surrounded on each side by small niches containing sculpture, and one over its pointed top, containing the sculptured image of the Madonna and child. In a city district of the Ottocento, a small hotel advertises itself with the graphic use of piles of cannonballs, arranged around its entrance. In the commercial streets of Venice signage is kept to a minimum; the graphic facade, more of a tradition, continues in use.

In visual terms, the amalgam of urban and architectonic forms with color is evident throughout Venice—the two are inextricably connected. Byzantine traditions may account for this in part. The role of color is primary in

7-8 Front to side, Venetian fascia

mosaics; tesserae of semiprecious stones and gold leaf are modular, and there is no distinction between color and form. The work of artisans, sculptors, and masons created the Venetian vernacular.

Painting continued to be considered part of interior architecture, even after the Venetian invention of oil painting made it possible to work on portable linen surfaces. The walls and ceilings of great buildings would have been considered incomplete in the High Renaissance without the monumental presence of imagery.

The formal combination of sculpture and architecture is a legacy of the Gothic, represented in Venice. Rome had Bernini, but his fountains are freestanding sculptural groupings; here the embellishment of Venetian facades, reflecting medieval traditions, made no distinctions among the mason, sculptor, and architect. Few urban examples remain extant elsewhere in the world

The integration of city form with its function anticipates the credo of Modernism. In fact, this built continuum in time better represents this achievement than do most modern cities. Venetian monuments, however grand their purposes, reflect human scale and embrace the human spirit. The arts, in their direct appeal to the senses, create a distinctive sense of place, of abiding urban identity.

The richness of Venice is exemplary in its material form. Expressive of its preeminence as a maritime city for centuries, its cosmopolitan and sophisticated citizens exuberantly celebrated their city through the development of its arts. It remains—a threatened legacy— as the world's environmental fortune; no documents can recount the experience of great civilizations as do the stones and imagery of their cities.

7-9 Clock Tower, Piazza San Marco

7-10 Hotel of the Ottocento, Venice

7-11 Rome, Baroque facade

ROME

The monumentality of Imperial Rome remains imprinted in the proportions of its facades. Massive and grounded, buildings here express grandness and gravitas. To the bulk of architectonic forms is added the optical weight of their color. Low on the Munsell scale, deeply saturated, yet at the same time rich and redolent of light, the colors of surfaces soften the severity. A sensuous human dimension is added to the facade, tempering the impact of formal grandeur.

In a city of mixed use, Roman facades are those of palazzi, domestic dwellings, shops, and cathedrals, within the same streets and districts. The imprint of the High Renaissance and Baroque marks the ample portals with heavy stone cornices, adorned with classical columns and architraves. Within portals, open patios are visible from the street, some ample enough to permit cars to park. Others display classical figures on pedestals, sarcophagi, and other sculptural fragments—icons of the ancient city.

At the terminals of streets, the rounded boundary of a great edifice is expressed in stone, carved curvilinearly to form the turn in direction. Rooflines are massive, overhanging the plane of the facade to the space of the

7-12 Baroque cornice

street. Balconies of marble or stone adorn windows. The baroque rhythm of stone interpenetrating space is carried into the palace or domestic dwelling. Architectonic function is articulated in a byplay of sculpture and light. Alternating curved with triangular architraves adorn the windows of a facade, forming a rhythmic grouping. On some streets color unifies a series of buildings of different ages, not by exact repetition, but within a grouping of adjacencies in hue, deep yellow to red-ocher to burnt sienna, to reddish umber, to a dry, raw umber. Rhythmic variations in the building planes, met by an equivalent use of color adjacencies in Roman facades, are characteristic of its vernacular.

Historic revisionism, which attributes gray neutrality to the ancient city, will deny the orchestration of Roman streets as color/formal continua. Far more subtle than the use of gray is this vernacular sensibility itself. The product of long observation of form and light and their integration with color, perceptual experience underlies these vernacular choices. They shape the urban field with a distinctive human imprint. Officialdom is associated with gray. The stones and marbles of church and governmental facades in their material structures may counterbalance the coldness of hue by inducing the byplay of light. Elsewhere color is human expression. Per favore, lasciare stare!

7-13 Via del Clementino, Rome

7-14 Facade, Via Condotti

7-15 Roman color adjacencies

7-16 Roman neutrals

7-17 Continuum of facades, Rome

7-18 Roman apertures

7-19 Central city, Rome

7-20 Pazzi Chapel, Firenze

FLORENCE

If Rome is replete with figurative imagery, then Florentine facades more abstractly encode their dimensions. Renaissance facades, sparing in narrative embellishment, are scaled proportionally, rather than depict to the human figure. Brunelleschi's Pazzi Chapel at Santa Croce, a model of Florentine architecture, achieves an equilibrium of measure. Visible in its entirety, the small building presents the vocabulary of colonnades, arches, walls. Within the interior, the cupola, floating by the support of its architectonic members, is a subtley orchestrated harmony of proportion. Restrained in carved detailing, the chapel's surfaces are expressed in a byplay of light and dark grays. Grace of intelligence, dignity, and lightness of bearing are conveyed by this architectural treasure.

Heavier Gothic influences in the city imprint their features on its facades. On the Via Turnabuoni, the palaces of the Medici and Strozzi retain some of the character of fortresses, their reticulated stone surfaces, weighty and somewhat forbidding, counterbalanced by the more graceful proportions of windows and portals.

Throughout Firenze the formal vocabulary of elegantly proportioned arches, architraves, generous windows, humane portals—the vernacular of Renaissance architecture —is evident. The practice of decorating exterior walls, facades, or open courtyards with painted ornamentation is a Florentine convention. The ceiling of the interior arcade within the Palazzo Vecchio retains gracefully painted arabesques. And near the Via del Arte della Lana, a wonderful Renaissance facade is painted with a fantasy of putti, griffins, and vines impaneled within ovals and rectangles that are fitted elegantly between the formal window apertures. Again, Florentine restraint prescibes a range of grays in coloration, achieving the expression of dignified celebration.

7-21 Bargello, Firenze

7-22 Palazzo Rucellai

7-23 Palazzo on the Lungarno

7-24 Oltrarno, Firenze

7-25 Via del Arte della Lana, Florence

7-26 Safed, facade

7-27 Synagogue at Safed, Israel

7-28 Hebron

ISRAEL

Throughout its history this ancient land has had many faces. The overlay of cultures one upon another has tended to efface their traces, and often only remnants remain embedded in the facades of its cities. Applied color designates, marks, or symbolically assigns; it is used sparingly. Fragmentary colors superimposed on its stones serve to signify the identity of the present inhabitants. In the Old City of Jerusalem often an aperture, or the colors surrounding it, will designate which sector of the city this is, perhaps the influence of an ancient Hebraic prescription "to place a sign on the door." In the Jewish quarter this will be designated with yellow; in the Arab sector blue or green will identify a place. Or the facade will be whitewashed, then painted with symbols of Mecca around or over the doorway.

7-29 Saturday morning, Bethlehem

Safed, the home of medieval Jewish mysticism, has an austere presence. The stone facade of a restored synagogue eschews decoration; the proscription against imagery permitting only spare incised symbols and calligraphy on lintel and aperture. On a domestic facade in the town yellow is painted in a fragmentary manner.

In Bethlehem, on the other hand, a newly constructed stone storefront has been entirely covered with light blue paint, an Arabic sign posted above the doorway. On a busy morning a barbershop, its iron front painted green, shows the frantic pace of human activity, before and behind the windowpane.

Hebron is a stone city; the ancient tombs of the Biblical patriarchs and matriarchs Abraham, Jacob, Isaac, Sarah, Rebecca, Leah, and Rachel are surrounded by buildings of more recent vintage, constructed of the same material. Squarely hewn whitish blocks, sharply articulated in the dazzling light, and the paradox of television antennas on rooftops bring the present into sharp focus.

7-30 Poor vendor's tableau in a Mexican market

MEXICO

In Mexico only the ruins of great Pre-Colombian civilizations remain, destroyed by the Spanish conquest. Written accounts at the time described the splendor of the Aztec city, including its color. Mayan temples and sculp-ture show traces of coloration, and surviving ceremonial ceramic vessels are painted, indicating that at the height of its civilization it was a major component of visual expression. In the remains of hue on stone monuments in the Yucatán, in the valleys of Mexico and Oaxaca, and on well-preserved Mayan ceramic pieces are found reds, yellows, and blacks, all oxides available from earth sources. Indigenous culture survived in the traditions of folk art, including the art of city color, in a culture of poverty. In crafting their folk arts, the taste of the indigenous people can be subtle. In weaving villages in Oaxaca serapes are woven with the restrained neutrals of natural whites, grays, browns, and blacks of wool fibers. Cotton and silk are still dyed with pigments available through natural sources. The cochineal worm provides a rich range of indigos to blues; plants and flowers produce rich reds and yellows. In the late nineteenth

7-31 Reconstruction of Aztec temple, National Museum of Archeology, Mexico, D.F.

century Germans introduced chemical dyes to Zapotecan weavers, causing an intensified and garish palette, uncharacteristic of their taste. Most of these blankets are sold to tourists.

Mestizo culture, or the mix of indigenous with Spanish influences, is dominant throughout Mexico. To ascribe the singular love of color displayed in Mexican towns and cities to a single source is problematic. Along with their settlements, following the conquest, the Spanish brought the arts of tile making and

ceramics, which thrive in practice in colonial cities today. The architecture of southern Spain, in turn, was influenced by Moorish traditions. In the Alhambra, the architectonic formalism, which combines structure and surface tiling and the fusion of color and form, found its highest, most sophisticated expression. Whether color usage in Mexico can be attributed to colonial influences is speculative.

More immediately influential on the vernacular eye than an imported tradition would be the existing fluorescence of *natural* forms in Mexico. The environment provides thousands of examples of color, expressed integrally with forms in their contexts. Iridescent hummingbirds, raucously colored toucans, bright parrots, butterflies of all descriptions, and flowering plants abide in astonishing variety in the rain forests. Invention in their patterning and coloration provides natural challenges to the human imagination when translated for use in the built environment.

Ancient Pre-Colombian sculptural traditions of indigenous origins used natural sources in their form and iconography. Plumed serpents, jaguar heads, and other animal features were often integrated with human forms in imagery. If the affinity for Nature's colors and forms compelled artistic innovations in Pre-Columbian architecture and sculpture, it is reasonable to assume that it would prevail in contemporary vernacular expression. In Mexico the love of color seems to be intrinsic, a vital, significant part of the collective psyche.

In the city of Mexico, D.F., a light recessive blue chosen for a noble building has a portal and window of heavy, carved stone as its facade. In Oaxaca de Juarez a building's face is painted violet adjacent to butterscotch; beneath the roofline the cast shadow reflects saturated red. A cadmium yellow facade surrounds an earth-pink window. Directly adjacent to it, the mauve wall of a shop declares its goods—suitcases, belts, ponchos, blankets, shirts, chaps, and pants. In Vera Cruz a facade in sharp light and shadow defines itself with the high contrast between dark green wall and bright red door. A coffee-cream building is made distinct against its bright orange neighbor. The wainscoting on the exterior of a convent in Puebla is a serious, dark brown, weighing heavily downward to settle the placement of a whitewashed wall—itself punctured by the simple, heavy rounded archway of the door.

Clarity and simplicity prevail in buildings. A doorstep to an entrance may be flush with the facade, but is articulated with a contrasting painted color. The overhang of a building is a flat horizontal projection from the roofline, signified by color. Front to side, orientation is expressed by a change from yellow to blue. The architecture of minimalism in a culture of poverty does the most with the least resources.

Contrasts in color define the edges of Mexican cities with the expansive sky. The towers of colonial churches are white, dazzling in adjacency with their dark red brick facades, and looking upward they intensify the blue field of sky. Bright light bounces and reflects beneath a balcony on a painted facade, reddening its pink surface in shadow. Fully saturated colors enliven Mexican shad-

7-32 Facade, Puebla

7-33 Facade, Vera Cruz

7-34 Facade, Oaxaca

ows in the brilliant, clear light of the region, in contrast to the neutrals that define shadows in less radiant northern cities.

When every surface is colored, combinations of brilliant colors that arrest the eye may occur by chance. On a street in Jalapa, Vera Cruz, a woman in magenta strides toward a building where its primary red facade in shadow contains the figure of a small girl in a bright orange dress. Or a green-lemon yellow VW "bug" appears parked before a butter-yellow wall. In Mexican towns exuberant expression seems to erupt spontaneously.

7-35 Convent in Puebla

7-36 Vera Cruz

7-37 Cathedral in Puebla

7-38 Mexico, D.F.

7-39 Mexico, D.F.

7-40 Facade, Vera Cruz

7-41 Taos, New Mexico

SANTA FE

Unlike Mexico, New Mexican facades are not colorful, except for the coloration of natural earth. In keeping with the indigenous Navajo Pueblo in the vicinity of Taos, the towns are more distinguished by the shapes of buildings than by their color. Given their small scale, and heights of one or two storeys, domestic buildings are simple volumes, adorned with wooden porches and apertures painted variants of sky blue or turquoise. The arcaded

passageways of storefronts, constructed of wood, are similarly painted so that throughout the city a cohesive sense of form and color prevail. In consequence, unity and continuity are the aesthetic effect.

Simplicity of volume and the spare usage of color in detailing create a field for the byplay of light and shadow. Adobe volumes, added like children's blocks one upon another, lend distinction to a hotel in Santa Fe, a mimetic recall of the Navajos' dwelling place. Glorious in the sunlight, its surfaces read as reddened, rich earth. Apertures in the plain walls are highly visible; as thin glass windows contrast with the thick adobe, they read as holes in this light. Exaggerated by the intensity of the Sun, the shapes of timbers protruding from the rooflines of houses cast sharp shadows against their facades. These repeat the rhythms of the indigenous Pueblo, where lean-tos provide shelter for the oven mounds built by the Navajos apart from their urban complex.

7-42 Santa Fe, New Mexico

7-43 Taos pueblo

7-44 Sunset Towers, Art Deco building, Los Angeles

7-45 Graphic facade, Venice, California

LOS ANGELES

Domestic architecture that derives from indigenous traditions, the white stuccoed and red-tiled roof dwellings of "Hispanic" influence, the California bungalow, pattern book architecture, or Modernist open-planned houses are examples of authentic vernaculars. Most districts of the city, however, are the work of developers rather than architects, and in these the appearance of a style was adapted as a "front" for a building. Streets in these places are formed as sequences of detached buildings, each styled differently—New England Colonial next to French Provincial, neither one imitated with much accuracy. A name is inscribed, added to the address, in digits large enough to be read from a passing car, to further identify the villa. This eclectic mix, a sequence of signs, presents false fronts; within, the apartments may be identical. That Americans move on average every 3 years is a possible message in the graphic housefront; best to continue advertising the place for rent.

Mansions on Sunset Boulevard may be as eclectic stylistically as their less-distinguished neighbors, providing the newcomer with the opportunity to shape or change his or her origins at will. The thinness of surface is therefore both a

7-46 Venice, California

conceptual and visual attribute, the projection of a mask, rather than a face.

Storefronts display the graphic facade to commercial advantage—direct advertising. More rapidly than signage, the architectural graphic is perceived from a moving vehicle and, therefore, serves a purpose. Individual imagination and creativity are manifested here with the mixture of styles. Melrose Avenue has distinct character—commercial, arty, hip, and self-aware. Rodeo Drive in Beverly Hills is cosmopolitan, understated, advanced in design, and visually similar to districts in Mexico City or European capitals. Los Angeles's Venice is a district in

the making—perhaps the most innovative in design and in the use of color on its facades.

Throughout, the medium is the message. The sign is primary in a visual culture adapted to speed and rapid recognition, where quick association equals cognition. Los Angeles is not the only city to express contemporary mercantilism on its facades, but it offers many examples. The communications capital of America now, once it was only Hollywood's movie industry. Perhaps similarity in the use of imagery over substance in the built environment can be compared with their TV commercials; they are hyperactive, brash, and artificially colored.

THE CARIBBEAN

On Barbados the vernacular predominates, for the small island in a region of light is inhabited by an indigenous population. Small frame houses dot the island; cabin-sized, one-family dwellings are simple, neatly maintained, and individually colored. Subtle colors are preferred on the facades, with contrasting details around window frames and doorways. Purple-brown with white and light blue frames on one, or sky blue facade with deep green details on another.

In Bridgetown the pink and blue facades associated with the Caribbean are seen on street

facades, but they are light, that is, high on the value scale, rather than bright, and nuanced, rather than saturated, in hue. The tendency for reflected light to bounce from the streets'

7-47 Barbados, house

7-48 Street in Vieques

7-49 Bridgetown, Barbados

surfaces back to the base of the facades adds the variant of saturated color, physically.

On Vieques, a tiny island off the coast of Puerto Rico, color usage on the facades of houses is more saturated than on Barbados. Here the detailing of wooden porches, and the framing of apertures with contrasting color, is also customary. A street on Vieques, located a few hundred feet from the Caribbean, is painted with a wide swath of blue, extended from curb to sidewalk and facade. Beyond, the sea is visible, startlingly similar in hue.

Trinidad's houses are embellished with the wide verandas and ample rooflines of colonial Indian influences, and are more richly colored than those of Barbados.

Graphic facades are a significant part of the culture of poverty. Absent other materials for display signage, paint is the least expensive way to decorate a building or to advertise its commercial purpose. In poor neighborhoods the custom of painting the face of the building to distinguish it from its neighbors, and to embellish it with symbols or lettering, is a universal vernacular expression.

Elegant, gracious, and stylish, the great lady reveals her distinction facially. Whether manifested in the formality of a town house or palace, or by a building in the market district, the aesthetic is one of dignified composure.

The posture of a grand hotel is large and serene. It sits solidly on its foundations and marks distinctions between functions clearly on its facade. The lower storey is ample and high, with a grand entrance and large windows. Distinct from the upper storeys, it is marked also by lighter coloration. French blue awnings shield the sunlight from tall windows; the rest of the embellishment is

sculptural—to play with the light. Cornices and balconies are articulated.

In keeping with its neighbors on the Right Bank, the stone surfaces are similar, but not identical in hue. A small variant in a neutral will keep the eye moving and prevent monotony in an understated urban environment. Stylistically similar, variation in rooflines and apertures offer distinction within limitations of heights and size of buildings. Streets of connected facades are similarly varied by subtle shifts in hue and variation in fenestration. Buildings are solidly grounded and substantial in volume, conferring both sobriety and

7-50 Parisian hotel

grace to this Parisian arrondissement. The Left Bank neighborhood is equally elegant. Facades are clearly articulated by changes in coloration. When painted, these are dark in value, indigos, varnished browns, raw umbers, blacks, or midvalue cool neutrals, in a range from blue-gray to tawny mixtures. Dark and recessive, these colors impart authority and restraint in a district containing art and antique galleries. Signage is large and clear against the storefront, inscribed in a variant of Diderot or period Roman lettering. The close range relationships of coloration and graphics in these facades impart a sense of unity to the district, rather than commercial competition. Restraint and refinement is the urban message.

The sematographic facade is found here as well. A four-star restaurant advertises its Style Nouveau facade, embellished in green with gilt detailing, its entrance a polished wood revolving door. The nineteenth-century atmosphere is preserved, rather than simulated, by architectural graphic style and color. In a market district the horse butcher advertising with a head over the doorway— sculpted and patinated in brass—of the real

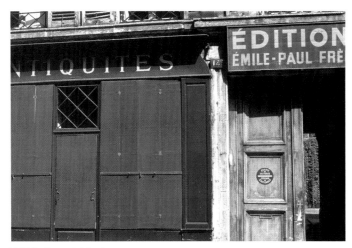

7-52 Bookstore, Left Bank

7-53 Storefront, Left Bank

thing completes the tableau with a clear primary red awning, white sans serif letters, and primary blue pillars and conveys the message. Unambiguously.

Clarity of exposition is a French characteristic, expressed in its written and spoken language. Visual articulation is also a Parisian attribute, evident in the physical environment. An abiding source, it may continue to shape its native population.

7-54 Parisian graphic facade

7-55 Sematographic, Paris market

7-56 Alpine facade

FRENCH ALPS

French color sensibility is reflected in an Alpine town, where the increased intensity of light causes luminosity in shadows. A house facade painted a rich rose-mauve resonates with warmth in shadow. To complement the low-valued intensity, bright chrome green has been chosen for its shutters. Such a resonant color relationship might have been expected in sophisticated Paris, but it occurs here on a very simple dwelling.

7-57 Town in French Alps

7-58 Lower Manhattan

anonymous. Moreover, within an increasingly dense grid, the probability of the surface of an entire building being noticed considerably diminishes, and with it any concern for its aesthetic effect. Ubiquitous concrete solves the problem of surface cheaply and quickly for the developer—and city walls vanish to the function of background.

The concept of the scaling of high rises existed when the city was less dense. In the 1920s setbacks created the hallmark pinnacles of Manhattan's skyscrapers. This innovation provided its distinctive urban edge when, looking upward, the culminating point of a building was seen silhouetted against the sky. At the same time, the designer Ely Kahn introduced the use of terra-cotta facing for skyscrapers, scaling their coloration from dark at the base to a light pinnacle to conform to the natural pattern of sun and shadow.

Color usage now is problematic, because expansive areas of neutrality in the urban field behave as extended background. Recalling the scene opening Woody Allen's film *Manhattan,* where the city skyline rolled horizontally across the screen, the image shot in black and white evoked the neutrals of the skyscrapers as if they had been recorded with color film.

The introduction of color on a single building can draw inordinate attention to itself, as the flashy aluminum skin on the Citicorp Building in the East 50s clearly demonstrates. Materials like reflective glass, or metals that shine, are irritants to the eye, adding visual to the existing aural cacophony of the city.

In the anonymous modern city, color is relegated to the entrances of buildings or to storefronts, relatively limited areas within the

NEW YORK, NEW YORK

Manhattan's forest of skyscrapers creates a collective impression, too numerous and densely packed now to reveal the identity of individual facades. Because the origins of a mobile population become insignificant in a cosmopolitan city, its buildings' faces also are

7-59 SoHo, New York

arc of vision. Examples of graphic facades are abundant; most in midtown Manhattan are corporate logos, but on Madison Avenue or downtown, in SoHo, sophisticated chains and independent shop owners embellish their store windows elegantly.

The storefront as signage *is* the Manhattan vernacular. In their small boutiques individual entrepreneurs imaginatively design the facade-as-tableau, using mannequins and the goods themselves as display. Graphics may be understated, as in the names of stores designed as small signatures on SoHo's facades. Occasionally a garish combination of gilt, bright apricot, and turquoise intrudes on an establishment aching for attention. But, on the whole, the facades are well designed, lettering and other graphic components are integrated in scale, and they are legible from a

7-60 East Village, Manhattan

distance and include the use of color more sparsely than in comparable districts in Paris.

Manhattan's filtered light, a function of its island geography and dense urban landscape— added to the hard surfaces from which sunlight bounces and scatters—presents a median level of light intensity to the eye. Whether native to the city or not, the visual system of a New Yorker is conditioned by this environment— and with it a consequent taste for, or avoidance, of color. But within these parameters, safe neutrality is not the only option.

7-61 Storefront, SoHo

7-62 Commonwealth Avenue, Boston

7-63 Back Bay, Boston

BOSTON

Boston's domestic character, produced by an architectural scale and tapestry of brick woven throughout its eighteenth- and nineteenth-century neighborhoods, is evident on its facades. The Back Bay is human in scale. Its town houses, connected in rows, express stability, and are individually defined by variation in the design of doorways, fenestration, and apertures and in the cultivation of small front gardens.

When designed, the urban plan for this area included these variants; nineteenth-century individualism was imprinted along with formality. Consistency in the coloration of the Back Bay, South End, and other Boston neighborhoods unify them. Throughout long, hard New England winters, sandstone and red bricks confer warm ambience to a

neighborhood. For the self-disciplined, pragmatic Yankee, the preference for stone and brick, permanent surfaces, crafted and modulated, is in evidence throughout the city. In the Back Bay and on the industrial waterfront, there are finely wrought examples of brickwork in a variety of textures and colors constituting the facades.

Eclectic formal elements tend to be unified by these surfaces. Bostonians who built the Back Bay were travelers, and the obligatory voyage to Europe yielded the mansard roofs of Paris and Italianate details on facades of mansions. The integration of these styles, however, was accomplished by limitations in building scale and the use of materials. In addition to brick, slate roofs, copper gutters, and stone details repeat in varied form throughout the district. The sense of hand craftsmanship is evident;

7-64 Facade in Back Bay

even when wooden cornices and trim were manufactured by machine and mass-produced by the nineteenth century, the carpenter's skill remained essential, as well as that of masons and stonecutters. A sense of touch remains in durable form in the crafting of facades, contributing to the perception of the city as a humane environment.

The old industrial districts, at Fort Point Channel and other wharfs, have been in the process of revision since the 1960s. Their handsome architecture was converted to new advantage—upscale housing, studios for artists and artisans, galleries, small businesses, and museums.

The life of the city, as well as the waterfront, will be affected by development after the completion of the massive new arterial, the "Big Dig." Control over the size, density, and ambition of future projects will require consideration of the scale and unique flavor of the old city. Like Boston's domestic districts,

7-65 Mansion, Back Bay

the wharf and industrial buildings here have their own visual character as they conform to limitations originally imposed on their height, size, and appearance. The integration and consistency of Boston's domestic and industrial districts has conferred upon it the image of a "city as a work of art." Restraint in the design and scale of future projects on its extensive waterfront and consideration for its unique urban character are called for to maintain Boston's essential distinctiveness.

7-66 Magdalene College, Cambridge University

BRITAIN

In the academic town of Cambridge the patina of time is left intact upon its facades. The blind windows of a stately facade are covered with soot and grime; an industrial veil articulates the relief of its detailing. A dark red wall, blackened by the accrual of microorganisms in this damp climate, contains the small bright feature of a yellow door. The bookstore, a graphic facade of half-timber construction, is a pattern of black and white.

The tawny stones of its colleges are cleaned and their medieval character maintained. The emblematic use of color at the entrance to Magdalene College is expressed by the polychromed sculpture of an enshrined Mary with heraldic beasts, in dark slate blue, dusty rose, and gilt. Time's patina, like varnish on an old painting, may have desaturated the red and blue, but the gold prevails. In the Middle Ages, color in heraldry assigned meaning and was intended to be read.

On the whole the stone of these ancient buildings is warm in coloration and within the middle range on the Munsell scale of values. In the town of Cambridge, however, facades are more frequently lower on the scale, dark red or gray bricks are prevalent. Storefronts may be of varnished wood, or painted indigo, with contrasting areas of light chrome green. Graphic signage is crisp and clear. When bright or saturated colors appear in this environment they occur in small areas. White window frames are graphic delineations. Occasionally, on doors, a primary color occurs; in the context of the dark environment a saturated blue door appears bright. But there is a preference for light, rather than bright, details, and the vernacular choices are more frequently subdued and understated in color.

7-67 Storefront in Cambridge, England

7-68 Barbershop, Cambridge

7-69 Shopfront in Old Town, Stockholm

7-70 Kallaren den Gyldene Freden, Stockholm

The special features of Stockholm, Old Town, are its light and the consistency of its physical environment. A sense of closure and containment is conferred by its small spaces and winding streets. The domestic facades are warm in coloration, ocher yellow contrasts with apricot; continuous rows of buildings are nuanced in articulation, defining property lines. The raking light on a shop etches its rough surface and skims the dark well of display window. On the shadowed side, a cigarette store is colored pre–World War II "Lucky Strike" green; a complementary red plane is seen adjacent through the window. This dark smokey green recurs on the face and shutters of a building, and again on a richly fenestrated doorway, trimmed electrically with orange. It reminds the eye of the weight of shadows, while containing warmth in its mixture.

Simple forms and heavy details characterize the town—a painterly place of strong contrasts and a range of colors, earthy and substantial, like the buildings themselves.

7-71 Facade, Copenhagen

COPENHAGEN

By contrast with its Swedish neighbor, Copenhagen feels more open, lighter, and more graphic than painterly in appearance. Continental stylishness characterizes the storefront; a red brick wall is punctuated by elongated windows and a small, curvilinear door that is painted a gray influenced by green.

Linearity characterizes the architecture of the old Bourse; its brick facade is penetrated with fenestration all along its extension. Dark red, the brick contrasts with the vertigris of the weathered copper roof, pinnacle, and gutters. The facades of the waterfront buildings are more widely contrasted in color and value than those of Stockholm. Light yellow against dark slate blue, whites and blacks contrasting with light blues, effect a northern palette.

8-1 Cave at Santa Clara, New Mexico

APERTURES

8

Urban form at intimate range—the opening in a facade, the place of entry, and the window—reveals an aperture that is spatially marked and identified ceremonially by form and color. The most expressive aspect of the architectural vernacular, it probably originated in primal form in the opening of caves.

Looking outward, an articulating boundary frames the vast panorama of the New Mexican sky and earth, while at the same time it defines the enclosure of the cave. For the Anasazi, this natural form provided both habitat and observatory, while the eloquent shape of the aperture mimics that of an open mouth.

At Jericho, near the Dead Sea, in the remains of the wall of a Crusader castle, an aperture, shaped like a keyhole, frames a view of the sea, its size and shape recalling that of the human body. Doorways in the walls of Mesa Verde, kept to minimal openings, also conform to human shape, wider at the head than at the threshold.

Although the arches of Roman amphitheaters were structural in function, their majestic remains seem to capture and enclose the sky. A metaphoric, as well as a physical, frame for the contemplation of nature, there is a connection between the Roman framing of space and the development of perspective as a science. The concept of perspective requires a fixed vantage point within the visual range of the human eye. A field that encompasses these spatial limitations, a frame of reference, ultimately the picture plane, begins with an aperture. The Roman arch may have served the human eye, as the viewfinder of the camera does now, to delimit the natural field.

The Renaissance invention of perspective defined a system, one based upon the objective placement and foreshortening of the figure in space, a Roman achievement. This classical invention set the stage for the Renaissance conception of a single, centric vanishing point, one-point perspective, or two points laterally placed on the picture plane, to which all linear boundaries would converge. Thus, within the parameters of a

8-2 Crusader castle, Dead Sea, Israel

8-3 Colosseum, Rome

8-4 Arch of Titus, Rome

self-contained surface, all figural elements seen in the visual field could be rationally related to one another in size and distance. A convincing illusion of "reality."

The ceremonial frame, an artifact of Venice, Rome, Bologna, and other Italian cities is a distinctive urban feature. Archways and arcades frame streets and open marketplaces, providing enclosure and shelter from wind and rain. In brilliant climates, like Jerusalem's, they are a refuge from the sun. As an architectonic device, a frame isolates one area of color from another, creating a break in the urban pattern. An arcade's enclosure intensifies urban color by scattering its light.

The significance of the aperture to the architecture of cities lies in the connection with identity, recognition, placement within a social hierarchy, or within the urban pattern itself. The gates to fortress cities, like ancient Jerusalem or medieval Siena, Lucca, or Cortona were clear signs of entry and symbolic ceremony, serving, as well, as points of orientation. Free-standing gateways, such as the Arch of Triumph in Paris, the Arches of Titus and Constantine in ancient Rome, or the Grand Army Plaza in Brooklyn, are significant as symbolic entrances.

In Japan the aperture as a freestanding gateway is a ubiquitous architectonic feature of great significance. The torii of the Shinto

8-5 Shinto shrine, Tokyo

8-6 Siena, Piazza del Duomo

shrines are rectangular standing elements, found throughout Japanese cities in sacred places. In Buddhist temple compounds great gateways, structures as elaborate as the temples themselves, function as ceremonial entrances. Spatial divisions, they may be combined with stairways, slowing the pace of a pilgrim on his or her way to the sacred shrine. Denoting a separation between urban and

sacred space, their ceremonial significance is repeatedly expressed in great works of art and architecture.

The freestanding gateway is a feature also of traditional Japanese domestic architecture. As one of a series of partitions, characteristic of this indigenous form, the entrance facing the street is shielded. In place of a facade, the

8-7 Artisan's shop, Cortona

8-8 Carpenter's shop, Venice

8-9 Ghiberti's bronze doors for the Florentine Baptistery

Japanese house is a series of screens, subsequent layers form interior spaces, which lead eventually to the enclosure of a garden. Within the vocabulary of forms particular to Japan, the aperture is one most richly conceived and integrated architecturally.

Apertures are notably absent in fortresses, except as emplacements for cannons or gun shafts. Blind walls are synonymous with bastions; monuments without windows or doors can be terrifying symbols of authority. Human identification with place may be enhanced by the parallels between windows and doors and the human features of eyes and mouth. On the human face, because expression depends on the vividness of these features, their coloration becomes singularly important. A staple device of the horror film is the colorless eye. On the other hand, soulful appreciations of dark or blue eyes have been the subject of countless elegies.

In places everywhere over the globe, I have observed the significance designated to the aperture. The primary distinction is structural, marking the distinction between plane and opening. The difference between the surface brightness of plane and darkness of opening, is next signified by a change in material color. The material shift is structural, that of stone facade to bronze or wooden door, from stone lintel to glass window, or adobe wall to wood frame. Materials themselves offer variations in color, altering with time and weather, as factored, or unintended, consequences, depending upon the culture.

The aperture offers the opportunity for design; elaborately embellished or plain,

8-10 Medici Palace, Firenze

8-11 Ca'd'Oro, Venice

8-12 Cambridge, England

8-13 Back Bay, Boston

even severe, the combinations of this basic form with its themes and variations appear to be nearly infinite. A function of economics, the embellishment may be sculpted, incised, ornamented with marble, stone, or bronze—

or simply painted. Marking the ceremony of entrance with color is as much a distinction made by cultures of poverty as it was that of princes. As expressive forms, they speak for themselves.

8-14 Taos pueblo, New Mexico

8-15 Bethlehem

8-16 Venice

8-17 Lucca

8-18 Santa Fe, New Mexico

8-20 Mexico

8-19 San Gimignano

8-21 Lucca

9-1 Chiles and spices, Mexican market

9-2 Birds, Mexican market

AT HUMAN SCALE

MARKETS

New York's Wall Street may be the world's first virtual market, but claims to the effect that the electronic exchange of goods and services will inevitably replace traditional markets are highly exaggerated.

The market represents humanity's most ancient and durable forum of congregation and exchange. In modern cities over the globe, central markets exist for the delivery of produce and comestibles of all kinds, and although nearly invisible in a major metropolis, their daily function is inextricably woven into the city fabric.

In more remote towns everywhere, local market days still draw people from their respective regions for the exchange of goods and services as well as for politics and gossip. The tangible experience of evaluating, by means of the eye, nose, and hand, the quality and freshness of produce is a human capacity being bred to extinction in "civilized" places. In fact, it is far *more* civilized to engage, with full exercise of the senses, in the evaluation and acquisition of

goods most fundamental to the basis of life than to relegate the issue to advertisers and their product labels.

Having evolved from a place that delivers the convenience and sanitation of packaged food to the arena of aggressive and repetitive advertising, the supermarket offers little real variety of products or sensory stimulation. Too often it smells of chemical detergents, instead of food, or worse, disinfectants to mask the handling of meat and fish. Not surprisingly, the local meat and fish market, the greengrocer, and the local market day are being revived in urban places. It makes an appearance outdoors in Union Square, Manhattan.

On the American continent the market had its origins in indigenous Mexico, and its survival there, through the Spanish conquest to the present, is testament to its importance. Elsewhere in the world, the market is essential to an understanding of vernacular culture and local color, not only because the truism, "you are what you eat" prevails, but because is the site of vernacular culture at its most basic. Food markets display the variety of

9-3 Bananas in Mexican market

locally grown produce, the herbs and spices that enhance the cuisine, the local fish in all its variety. A total sensorium to the experienced eye, the appearance of comestibles is clue to their freshness and flavor, but the heft of a fruit tells of its ripeness, and an "off" smell of fish or meat is not to be ignored. Shopping in a native market, moreover, draws one closer to people; the exchanges that take place, while brief and focused, are communal. Farmer's markets remind the consumer that hard work is required to grow food, and that simple conversational exchange befits giver and receiver. Repeated experience also educates. Ancient orchards in New England grow varieties of apples, and their flavors, that never appear in stores. Local delicacies or versions of familiar vegetables introduce variety to the diet. And the flavor of corn, picked and cooked the same day, is a marvelous, simple delicacy, a celebration of summer's brief season, the experience, by taste, of the Sun and the Earth.

Although markets are universal, everywhere they differ. The presentation of a stack of oranges in a pyramid, an example of the universal principle of the close packing of spherical shapes, can be seen in any market.

The color of chiles and spices, and their careful arrangement as rows of small hills, is Mexican. The juxtaposition of parrots, for sale in cages, with feather dusters made from the remains of their cousins, reflects Mexican experience. Here life and death can occur rapidly in sequence, and the culture faces the presence of this daily reality with vivid expression. Cakes baked in the shapes of skeletons are made for children on the Day of the Dead, in Oaxaca. The variety of bananas and plantains in the Mexican market offers a range of green, yellow, and red fruits in shapes that are broader and more abundant than any seen elsewhere—a legacy of the tropics.

In Venice the great variety of seafood from the nearby Adriatic is displayed in the daily market in highly varnished and cleaned bins, open to the discerning eye. Their shapes remind one of the sculpted reliefs found on the facades in the city. A skatelike fish is displayed next to its cleaned and splayed version. Live eels on a box are shown next to a skinned and cleaned specimen, shown in the position of swimming. Exuberance and a hearty love of food are expressed in this market, which is kept scrubbed down and scrupulously clean in the daily ritual of its presentation.

The presentation of food is key to a culture's values. In Paris fish are neatly layered in orderly rows, separated by category. Flowers as set bouquets in pots, in harmonic displays of color, show restraint and refinement.

In a local market in Kyoto, the Japanese sister city to Paris, varieties of fish are placed adjacent to one another in small compartments. Pickles, fruits, and vegetables are arranged by contrasting color for display. A Japanese genius for packaging creates a design genre of its own. Literally anything bought, whether in an elegant store on the Ginza or in a simple neighborhood market, is meticulously, often ingeniously, wrapped.

In a Roman market, at the Campo dei Fiori, a lively display of pumpkins and gourds replays the color of its surrounding facades. A store shows cruciferous vegetables mixed with eggplant nearly prepared for ingestion, a baroque mix. The great variety of shapes given to Roman breads in a store window repeat the theme of visual abbondanza. At the same time, in specialty shops, the huge variety of cheeses and sausage available in Italy are given elegant presentation. The Italian love of good food and wine is another sign of its culture, fully alive and sensuous, and celebrated as an art form.

9-4 Central Market in Venice

9-5 Adriatic fish, whole

9-6 Adriatic fish, splayed

9-7 Eels in a box, Venice

9-8 Parisian market

9-9 Adriatic shellfish

9-11 Kyoto market

9-10 Street market in Kyoto

9-12 Market at Campo dei Fiori, Rome

9-13 Roman market

9-14 Roman bakery

MATERIALS

A significant source of architectonic color is natural material. The use of stones and marbles in antiquity had its basis in availability—local quarries were nearby sources. But the stability of these materials were preferred also for their duration; buildings then were constructed for posterity, and indeed many have outlived their cultures. The preference for restrained neutrals, which natural materials offer, lies in their passivity; they permit volumetric architectonic forms to dominate as structures and in spaces.

A more subtle effect ensues, however, and one absent in most discourse concerning color in the built environment. The neutral appearance of stones has its cause in the quality of ambient light. When sunlight emanates directionally, from an angle, it illuminates the crystal structure of stones, marbles, and alabasters in unique ways. Light *physically* is color. The byplay of light within crystals, by reflection and refraction, itself elicits color changes. When crystals themselves contain hues, the range of possible colors, additionally mixed, becomes manifold. To the eye these mixtures are both vibrant and subtle because they respond to, and are conditioned by, light's natural fluctuations. These effects were appreciated in medieval and Renaissance Italy, where marbles and stone, some chromatic in details, were used to construct their churches and monuments.

This point was illustrated earlier in "Light, Surface, and the Environment" in Chapter 1.

9-15 Tufa, Segesta

9-16 Stone of the Sinai

9-17 Stone of San Gimignano

The columns of Greek temples in the luminosity of morning light show amber and violet coloration, a function of ambient light and consequent shadow. The limestones of which the city of Jerusalem is built respond as color both physically and perceptually, so that surfaces throughout the ancient environment undergo magical transformations, by exposure to the light of the region, the season, and the time of day.

Adobe is simply baked mud; its use integrates the color of the built with the natural environment. In the immense field of New Mexico with its intense ambient light, the transformations of light and shadow register as color variants, both physically and visually.

Bricks vary in coloration and shape, regionally and by age. The thin, elongated dry brown Roman brick is revealed in the Colosseum, absent its marble fascia. In New England bricks are yellows, oranges, browns, and varieties of reds, from light to dark.

Applied color is no less natural when its chemical sources are those of the Earth. Technology has expanded the chemical palette for artists' pigments, yet the predominance of iron oxides as yellows, reds, and browns are more in evidence in the cities reviewed here than the use of harsher artificial colors. The polychrome remains of Pre-Columbian, Mesoamerican cities show traces of earth color resources.

Better understood, coloration in the built environment could come to be regarded as an extension of natural structure. A more

9-18 Roman bricks, Colosseum

9-19 Boston wharf

comprehensive, scientific understanding of materials themselves would enhance and enlarge the discourse. Furthermore, in this age of technology, the issue of surface color as an artifact of microstructure presents an original challenge. A collaboration between microengineers and designers might produce new industrial surfaces of materials like those of crystals, responsive to light, for use in skyscrapers. However, intuitively and over time in the vernacular, the use of color responds to the need and reflects the significance of both the psychological power and the effect of this sensory dimension on the human spirit.

9-20 Detail, mosaic floor, San Marco, Venice

9-21 Detail, Trajan column, Rome

9-22 Detail, Manhattan

9-23 Watts Tower, Simon Rodia, Los Angeles

9-24 Ca'd'Oro, Venice

9-25 Ceiling, Central Market, Venice

9-26 Bronze doors, San Marco, Venice

DETAILS

Finally, the detail—the epitome of a culture. It appears as a tableau in the market, a fragment of carving or intarsia in a facade, a door handle. A chance event, the mark of individuality in place, it takes place in cities. Unplanned, an amalgam of details are visual events that, added together, constitute the psychological or local color of a city. They cannot be planned or designed, they merely occur as spontaneous expression; the older the culture, the more probable the frequency.

9-27 Doorhandle, Venice

9-28 Detail, church in Acatepéc

9-29 Doorhandle, Venice

9-30 Alpine cemetery

9-31 Detail, baptistery, Siena

9-32 Street shrine, Venice

9-33 Carved relief, Back Bay, Boston

9-34 Detail, shrine at Chion-in Temple, Kyoto

9-35 Detail, Giotto's Tower, Firenze

EPILOGUE

The urban features that rich and complex cities provide were not all designed and most were not built in one generation. Most cities today grow haphazardly and, unfortunately, without regard to those components that make them humane places. The mantra of "bottom line" has come to dominate all discourse, whether appropriate to the situation or not. Quick, cheap, and utilitarian have become building standards, and aesthetics have been redefined as "elitist."

Evidence to the contrary exists in all vernacular places that I have visited. The need for color, light, physical organization, and coherence is basically a human one, without reference to class or ethnicity. On the contrary, in the poorest neighborhoods a sense of beauty exhibits incipient artistic expression. Rather, greed lurks beneath this rhetoric. The rich and powerful from Byzantine and Renaissance Europe to nineteenth-century America were patrons of the arts, spending their wealth not only to embellish their own habitats, but also to build civic places and institutions. Cities at one time were built for the future; there was a sense that temporal values were transitory, and that future generations would benefit from the establishment of permanent monuments and urban complexes. That such places exist is cause for celebration, a legacy as well as a challenge to present standards.

There is a vital link between aesthetics and function; when the bottom line becomes the holy message, aesthetics are attacked, while at the same time the systems of civic functioning, infrastructure, and education are shamefully neglected. When aesthetic values are regarded as relics, and the sense of beauty, display, or embellishment are descried as "decorative values," is this evidence of deep seriousness in discourse or a quasi-totalitarian rejection of the human spirit?

Essentially the human need for beauty, order, and completeness is a spiritual one. The progenitor of the modern city was the sacred place. However complexly time has reshaped and eroded them, a sense of civilization abides only when these basic human conditions are met within the physical characteristics of cities. Visual attributes, form and color, were once considered essential components of cities. Old cities exemplify their cultures; they can be "read" more directly than texts and they reveal what the culture considers significant.

That color arises in an environment as a form of vernacular expression is an example and challenge for the designer. To correlate color as a shaping factor, within the physical constraints of a spatial order and its natural setting, requires analysis and sensitivity to context, the primary requisites for design.

The aesthetic city, the city of light, remains either a historical artifact or a human aspiration. Yet Nature abounds with aspects of display, embellishment, and sheer and ravishing *beauty*. Function is cleaved with aesthetics often in natural design. Despite all the brilliance of human engineering, we have yet to design an airplane wing as supple and agile in flight as the hawk's wing, or anything rivaling its beauty. In addition to its aerodynamic efficiency, at the level of its microstructure, the cells of wings are designed to reflect light as *color*. Functional? Possibly, as a natural visual code. To the human eye—aesthetic.

Perhaps it is time to reevaluate the meaning of function in design by embracing aesthetics as an essential part of forming the environment. Models exist.

COLORS GROUPED
BY CITY

VENICE

ROME

SIENA, CORTONA, BOLOGNA

ISRAEL, MEXICO

PARIS

STOCKHOLM, COPENHAGEN

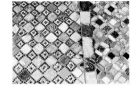

VENICE

ROME, LUCCA

FLORENCE

MEXICO, SANTA FE, CARIBBEAN

PARIS, FRENCH ALPS, STOCKHOLM

JAPAN

GLOBAL POSITION OF CITIES

Position on the global grid of cities studied: from North to South.

City	Latitude	Longitude
Stockholm, Sweden	59° 20′ N	18° 3′ E
Copenhagen, Denmark	55° 40′ N	12° 35′ E
Cambridge, England	52° 12′ N	0° 7′ E
London	51° 30′ N	0° 7′ E
Paris, France	48° 52′ N	2° 20′ E
French Alps	45 $\frac{1}{2}$°	6 $\frac{1}{2}$°
Venice, Italy	45° 27′ N	12° 21′ E
Florence and Tuscany	43° 46′ N	11° 15′ E
Rome	41° 54′ N	12° 29′ E
Boston, Massachusetts	42° 22′ N	71° 3′ N
New York, New York	40° 42′ N	74° 0′ W
Santa Fe, New Mexico	35° 41′ N	105° 57′ W
Los Angeles, California	34° 3′ N	118° 15′ W
Tokyo, Japan	35° 42′ N	139° 46′ E
Kyoto	35° 40′ N	135° 45′ E
Jerusalem, Israel	31° 46′ N	35° 14′ E
Mexico, Districto Federal	19° 24′ N	99° 9′ W
Vera Cruz, Mexico	19° 12′ N	96° 8′ W
Oaxaca	17° 3′ N	9° 43′ W
Barbados, Caribbean	13° 6′ N	59° 37′ W

BIBLIOGRAPHY

Albers, Josef. *The Interaction of Color.* New Haven: Yale University Press, 1963.

Arendt, Hannah. *The Life of the Mind.* New York: Harcourt Brace Jovanovich, 1978.

Burckhardt, Jacob. *The Civilization of the Renaissance in Italy.* Great Britain: Phaidon Press, 1950.

Charney, J. G. "The Dynamics of Long Waves in a Baroclinic Westerly Current," *Journal of Meteorology,* 1947.

Charney, J. G. "On the Scale of Atmospheric Motions," *Oslo Geofysiske Publikasjoner,* 1948.

Fitzpatrick, G. L., and Modlin, M. J. *Direct Line Distances,* International Edition. Metuchen, N.J., and London: Scarecrow Press, 1986.

Friedman, Mildred. *Tokyo Form and Spirit.* Minnesota: Walker Art Museum; New York: Abrams, 1986.

Goethe, Johann. *Theory of Colors.* London: J. Murray, 1840.

Jacobs, Jane. *The Death and Life of Great American Cities.* New York: Random House, 1961.

Katz, David. *The World of Color.* London: Kegan Paul, 1935.

Lynch, Kevin. *Image of the City.* Cambridge, Mass.: MIT Press, 1960.

Lynch, Kevin. *A Theory of Good City Form.* Cambridge, Mass.: MIT Press, 1982.

McAndrew, John. *The Open Air Churches of Sixteenth Century Mexico.* Cambridge, Mass.: Harvard University Press, 1965.

McCoy, Esther. *Five California Architects.* New York: Reinhold, 1960.

Minnaert, M. *The Nature of Light and Color in the Open Air.* New York: Dover, 1954.

Mumford, Lewis. *The City in History.* New York: Harcourt Brace, 1961.

Mumford, Lewis. *The Culture of Cities.* New York: Harcourt Brace, 1938.

Munsell, A. H. *A Grammar of Color.* New York: Van Nostrand Reinhold, 1969.

Rudofsky, B. *Architecture without Architects.* New York: Doubleday, 1964.

Ruskin, John. *The Stones of Venice.* New York: John Wiley, 1880, vol. 2, pp. 267, 386.

Sacks, Oliver. *The Island of the Color Blind.* New York: Vintage, 1996.

Schiller, Friedrich. *On the Aesthetic Education of Man.* New Haven: Yale University Press, 1954.

Scully, Vincent. *The Earth, the Temple and the Gods.* New Haven: Yale University Press, 1979.

Steiner, George. *Real Presences.* Chicago: University of Chicago Press, 1989.

Swirnoff, L. *Dimensional Color.* Boston, Basel: Birkhaüser, 1989; New York: Van Nostrand Reinhold, 1992.

The New York Times Atlas of the World. New York: Random House, 1993.

Wechsler, Lawrence. "L.A. Glows," *The New Yorker,* 23 February and 2 March 1998, pp. 90–97.

INDEX